Your Life is Calling

HOW TO **DO YOU**

AND LIVE WITHOUT REGRETS

ENE OBI

ISBN: 978-1-948777-23-0

Printed in the United States of America

About the Author

Ene Obi worked for global, corporate organisations for almost three decades, two of which in Human Resources. She has experienced, both personally and professionally, women who feel stuck and unfulfilled, struggling with a lack of clarity. Some are disillusioned with a stalling career while some want to experience something different after an accomplished career. Others have raised children who are now grown-up and they want to reconnect with the goals and dreams they put on hold. The reason may vary but the result is the same, they feel stuck, they want something more. They know that they have not exhausted their potential. There's an itch in their heart which leaves them asking, 'Now what?' Like any other itch, there's an uncontrollable urge to scratch.

Ene was one of these women. She had a thirst for something different. She wanted to use more of her skills and talents so she combined these with her passion and experience. That led her to set up Ziano Mindspa, helping women reconnect with their deeper selves, rediscover their greatness and develop a renewed sense of purpose.

Ene is on a mission to use her gifts, talents, and experiences to make a positive impact on as many people as she can reach. She is passionate about helping women discover all of who they are, see their full potential, and navigate a path to step into their greatness. She inspires women to give themselves permission to reach for their dreams so they can live a fulfilled life with no regrets.

In this book she shares the lessons and principles which helped her re-ignite the passions, dreams, and desires that had long been buried deep inside of her. It is a roadmap, connecting you from where you are to the possibilities of who you can be. Prepare to be empowered to write the next chapter of your life, this time with you holding the pen.

Stay in touch with Ene via:

- Website: https://www.ziano.co.uk
- Instagram: https://www.instagram.com/ziano_mindspa
- Facebook: https://www.facebook.com/ene.obi.7
- LinkedIn: https://www.linkedin.com/in/eneobi/

Contents

———

Preface

This book has been written for a global audience.
However, the spellings of words are based on British English.

The Lotus flower (on the front cover of this book) is a symbol of
miraculous rebirth, re-bloom and re-emergence.

Dedication

———

I dedicate this book to my parents,
Elisha Abumere Omokhodion and Lillette Omokhodion
(nee McDonald).

I also dedicate this book to my husband, Henry Obi
and sons, Karl Obi and Andre Obi.
You are my light.

To all the amazing people who helped make
this book a reality – Thank you.

To my family and friends who have supported and
encouraged me on my journey – Thank you.

Endorsement

———

If you are tired of feeling stuck in an unfulfilled life, if you're fed up with thinking the results in your life depend on something other than you, Your Life is Calling is the book for you.

In this book, Ene Obi shows it is possible to find and discover a new you, a new life greater than you ever thought possible. The amount of time and energy she has poured into this book are evident on each and every page you read. Each chapter is filled with the blueprint to create a completely new you. The first chapter is one filled with insights into who we think we are and the awakening to understand you are capable of so much more. The magic of the pen will allow you to write the next chapters of your life.

Ene has a very direct and straightforward approach on how to tap into your human potential and success. You will learn to identify the things that are holding you back from stepping into your greatness. Ene gives you the knowledge and understanding that can truly transform all you've ever wanted to be.

Each chapter is filled with inspirational and magical quotes from the legends of history that match the wisdom in each lesson. The "spa" at the end of the lessons provides an amazing location for you to visit your true self. The questions and exercises are the perfect treatment to master your mind and connect your inner and outer worlds to that untapped passion, purpose and possibility that exists within us all.

Ene peels back the layers of her awakening and holds nothing back as she shares that defining moment where she said no more to a life of simply existing and said yes to life of joy and happiness. She shares how you can take any perceived failure and discover that within that moment, a seed of success is planted for those willing to move forward along a path they've never taken before. The garden of the mind contains the rich soil to grow a new life, nurtured and guided by you.

The keys to transform and change your life, to master your thinking, your actions and your behavior can all be found in the following pages. She shows us that the starting point on the path to the life we desire all begins with gratitude and acceptance.

This new path continues to be created on a daily basis but it is now being constructed by the most talented and powerful architect on the planet, you.

When you make the decision to "Do You" as Ene says, you connect to the right kind of thinking, actions and results that you desire.

This book will open your mind to what is not only possible but what is necessary for you to share your beauty, magnificence and gifts to the world.

Jon Talarico
Founder, Master Your Mind

Foreword

———

If you have followed my career or heard me speak then you've often heard me say- "You have GREATNESS in you!"

It's a true statement that has deep power; however, for some of us, it's a truth that feels out of reach.

Life and circumstances can cause us to feel deflated, rejected, and perhaps, even worse - content with living a life that does not nearly reflect our inner greatness.

Instead, our lives can reflect pain, confusion, anxiety, fear, and other people's expectations of us.

If I had adopted the story that others told me about my life, I would still believe that I wasn't good enough to make my dreams come true. In fact, had I not found mentors, guides, and coaches who saw my greatness when I didn't, I may have never even dared to dream.

I had a calling on my life, but I would have missed it if I allowed myself to remain trapped inside of "just good enough."

I want you to know that I am not the exception to any rule. We each have something special within us that the world needs. It's our responsibility to discover that gift and share it.

It's true, we all have a calling on our lives.

Are you about to miss yours?

In Your Life is Calling, Ene Obi provides the principles and strategies required to focus your energy, mindset, and your direction on hearing and understanding your calling.

Many of us settle for a scripted life, where we believe we have to get a good job and work to survive. We never realize that there can be more. Ene and I are here to tell you... there's so much more in store for you!

A job (journey of the broke) is what you get paid for, a calling is what you're made for. A calling is something you love so much you'll do it for nothing, but you do it so well people will pay you to do it!

You might ask, what are the signs that life is calling you, Les?

Often, our calling speaks to us through what we experience as chaos and disruption. This was the case for Ene. In a situation that could have made her feel defeated, instead, Ene was finally freed up to hear the call!

It was as if a light switched on for Ene.

I have personally worked with Ene and I know that she is a woman on a mission to elevate the world! This book is a testament to her desire.

I am proud to call Ene my mentee and I am certain that if you apply the tools and techniques that she shares, you will not only hear that Your Life is Calling, but you will be compelled to answer.

The rest of the world will thank you!

Yours in GREATNESS,

Les Brown
Speaker, Author, Trainer

Introduction

T hink about your life as a book, with different seasons split into chapters. You've had some great seasons and you've probably had some not-so-great seasons.

You have achieved success, whether personally or professionally, but you know you haven't exhausted your full potential. You want to discover all of who you are and live a life with no regrets. You are ready to step up to your next level so you can live life in the fullest expression of yourself. You've come so far and you've done so much already, but you don't want to live the rest of your life or leave this earth only having done what you've already done. You didn't come this far to only come this far. You're saying, 'Don't hold me to what I've already done; hold me and help me become who I was destined to be.'

Deep inside of you, there is a desire for more. It may have started as a silent yearning in your heart but soon grew into a deafening ache for fulfillment. It is disruptive yet unrecognisable and unclear so you don't know where it's from or what it's saying. You're left feeling frustrated, empty and stuck. You feel drained, yet you know there is so much untapped potential in you. I know that feeling because for many years that was me.

The yearnings are coming from your heart. They're coming from a place where your goals and dreams have been buried. The desires you haven't yet explored. The ones you've talked about and dreamt about that you have since forgotten about. Perhaps you've told yourself the time isn't right. You've told yourself you'll do something about it when your circumstances change—maybe when you get a job, or leave a job, or when your children leave home, or when they come home. 'When' is sometime in the unknown future. The best time is now; there will never be a better time. Do it now!

As we go through life, we sometimes lose connection with who we are. We lose sight of our natural God-given talents, we lose sight of our skills, we lose sight of our dreams, we lose sight of what we love, we lose sight of ourselves. This leaves us feeling trapped, lost, and frustrated, living a life we don't love—a life we feel we have no control of. The result is misery, hopelessness, and powerlessness.

Sometimes we think we've got all the time in the world so we put our lives on hold and we stop dreaming. For some people, it becomes too late. They realise too late. They get to an age where they look back on their life and say, 'How did I spend my time on earth?' They realise they didn't give themselves a chance to reach their full potential. They didn't do many of the things they were capable of, things they wanted to do, things that set their souls on fire. They played it safe. Or worse, they didn't play at all. But it's too late for them.

This life is not a dress rehearsal, it's the real thing. It's real life. We get one chance and one chance only. As the saying goes, 'It's not the years in your life that counts. It's the life in your years'. Some lucky people realise this before it's too late, and they get a second chance or maybe even more chances.

Sometimes we put our identity in our work, in our family, or anywhere we can. Sometimes life events sway us off course and we keep our dreams and our passions on hold. They often come back to haunt us, though. Like a rubber ball that you try to suppress under water, they keep bobbing back up, looking for expression in our lives. The more we try to suppress them, the more they bob back up, until the energy spent in keeping them down becomes so great that we get tired and emotionally frustrated. It is this frustration that manifests itself as feelings of unfulfillment, entrapment, and discontentment. Our dreams go somewhere to die, taking with them our unused talents, gifts, and abilities.

If any of this resonates with you, you're in the right place. Consider yourself one of the lucky ones. You have taken the first step: identifying that your race is not over yet. They say that whenever you wake up is your morning. This is your morning. You are not too late; you're right on time, right where you need to be. This is your time.

In this book, be prepared to be taken on an inspirational journey with powerful quotes, poems, and lessons to help you rediscover your goals and dreams for your next season. Be inspired to reignite your lost spark and give yourself permission to break free. Be empowered to redefine yourself and stop being viewed by your relationships, circumstances, titles, or past failures.

At the end of each chapter is a *Spa*, with call-to-action prompts and exercises. Use these as an opportunity to reflect, explore your feelings, and identify any further action required by you. Your heart knows what you want and it is waiting for you to start. This time, you're the one holding the pen, so you can create the life you desire. You're ready for a breakthrough. All you need to do is give yourself permission.

'But', you say, 'I don't know what to write in the next chapter; I'm stuck! That's why I've been re-reading my current chapter'. Well, that's why you're here, at the Spa! Shut out distractions from the outside world, connect with your deeper self, and start writing. Don't worry about what to write, just pick up the pen and the words will flow.

Here's the best thing – you don't have to know where this next chapter is going. You just have to start dreaming it and when you do, write it out. They say that the best dreams happen while we're awake.

The Inner Sanctuary, which is at the end of the book, is my favourite part! Here you will find powerful, practical tools to help spur your inner power into action and bring about significant change to create the life you desire. If the book were a delicious meal, *The Inner Sanctuary* would be the wonderful, indulgent dessert at the end.

I ask two things of you:

First, to read this book with an open heart. Remember that you are at the Spa, so shut out distractions from the outside world and let your heart take over. Your head sees the past and the present and your heart sees the possibilities. As you read this book, open up the tap of possibilities.

Second, write your thoughts, dreams, and desires in the journal which accompanies this book. If you haven't got the accompanying journal, use the most beautiful journal you can find, as well as the most elegant writing pen.

Prepare to be rejuvenated, to reignite your lost spark, and to create the next chapter of your life. You're holding the pen, you're writing the story. You're the author of your story and the hero of your life.

Creating the next chapter of your life is a journey, not a destination. Enjoy the journey. Do not worry about the promised pot of gold at the end, because this journey is paved with diamonds.

Remember, you're not late, you're right on time. Your time. How would you start? What story would you write?

"Whatever you are seeking is also seeking you."
- Rumi

CHAPTER ONE

Know You

The Magic Pen

I magine you are given a beautiful pen. It fits perfectly in your fingers and writes smoothly. You're told that beauty is not the only attribute of this fine pen. It is a magic pen, custom-made for you, and whatever you write with this pen becomes real. Because of its magical powers it has only one purpose: to be used to write the story of your life from today onwards. Your job is to think about your life and take the story from here, creating the next chapter as you would like it to be.

What story would you write?

Would you write about your failures, past mistakes and pains?
Would you keep nailing yourself down in chains?
Would you say, I stumbled, I fell, beaten and broken
Confused, lost, weary and shaken
I felt I was worthless, laden with defects

Until a voice said, your imperfections make you perfect
You are unique with your scars and your bruises
For without them you couldn't fulfill your uses
Your voice, your strength, your past are your powers
That give you wings to share your story of conquer
A student of life, I wore the crown with glory
Now with my pen, I get to write my own story.

Ene Obi

Knowing that you are the author of the story that runs your life, how would you write your story?

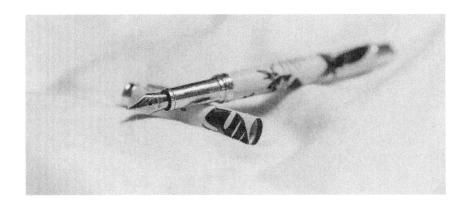

"Write the vision and
make it plain."
- Holy Bible, KJV, Habakkuk 2:2

Find Your Map

'Where I am going to is closer than where I am coming from'.

This was one of my dad's favourite sayings. It was a source of much amusement and laughter when I was younger, with my whole life still ahead of me. I'd see adults shake their heads in despair whenever my dad said this statement. I was oblivious to its deeper meaning. I no longer am, I now understand its meaning. Dear reader, this statement is a call to action.

Let me help you understand. What my dad was saying was that the road he'd travelled in his life to get to where he was at that moment was longer than the road he had ahead of him. Or, in the words of the legendary motivational master, Les Brown, 'The journey that I have travelled up to this point is longer than the journey that I have left'.

You get to an age in life when you realise that you have a shorter journey to the end of your life than from the beginning of your life to where you are right now.

I don't believe it is just the reality of their mortality that made people so desolate when they heard this statement. I believe it is also the stark realisation that they had not done the things that gnawed away in their hearts.

"Life is God's gift to us.
What we do with it is our gift to God."
- A.R. Bernard

They have not fulfilled their dreams, and in their hearts are mixed emotions of strong desires tinged with deep regrets. They don't want to die before they've lived but they know they're running out of time. Think about your goals and dreams and the things you want to do with your life. A lot of people put their dreams on hold, believing that they have time. Are you one of those people? Do you know how much time you have?

The world has been in the grip of a global pandemic that seems determined to cause colossal devastation. The Covid-19 pandemic is causing death, destruction, loss, and suffering. This deadly virus has ravaged the world for over a year and is responsible for over two million casualties worldwide as of January 2021. The infection and death data has evolved from anonymous numbers called out in regular government updates to names and faces of people. Real people. People you know or know of. Many people I speak to have directly or indirectly been impacted by the human loss of life due to Covid-19.

Virtually all parts of the world have spent weeks or months in one form of lockdown or another. We have had to adapt to new ways of working, become familiar with parts of our homes that we never knew existed, learn about our own family members in ways we might not have expected, and even attend parties virtually! This is not to mention the new words that have been added to our vocabulary: 'support bubble', 'lockdown', 'social distancing', 'flattening the curve', 'new normal', 'contact tracing', 'PPE' and many more. We have a common language; these words and phrases have become familiar to us and exist in even casual conversations.

"Time is a virtue."

The world has kept itself entertained (virtually, of course) with jokes and memes being circulated, providing light relief in uncertain times.

The virus has forced us to discard habits and circumstances that no longer serve us. It has helped us develop an agile response and create for ourselves a 'new better' instead of a 'new normal'. It has also given us the opportunity to reflect, reboot, and reset our life priorities. We are experiencing unprecedented and unpredictable times unlike any we've ever seen. We even have to be mindful of the very air that we breathe. Covid-19 has reminded us of the reality that we each have an expiration date which doesn't often announce its arrival.

So I ask again, how much time do you think you have left? What dreams have you put on hold? We need to act with a sense of urgency and become more purposeful in how we approach life. Use the time you have because time is the lifeblood of life. What you do with the time you have left on the planet determines how much value you place on the time you've been given.

"The wealthiest spot on the planet is the cemetery.
Because buried in the cemetery are dreams that were never fulfilled,
books that were never written, ideas that never became reality,
visions that were never manifested, paintings that were never painted,
sermons that were never preached, songs that were never written.
The cemetery is pregnant with unused success. Buried in the
cemetery is treasure that makes God weep."
- Dr Myles Munroe

The adage 'time is money' is true. Time is a currency; therefore, it can be spent, used, and invested. It can also be lost, wasted, abused, and squandered. Time is a limited resource which cannot be refunded or recovered. We have a finite amount of time on earth. Let every moment count.

This lesson was brought home to me on the sidelines of a rugby pitch where I spent a lot of time when my sons were younger. They played rugby for their school and football (soccer) for their school as well as outside of school, for a Sunday league club called Parkfield. The parents would go to matches to support their sons and the team. In those days we used camcorders to record special moments; I don't think smart phones with video recording function were available. If they were, we certainly weren't using them the way we're using them now.

Anyhow, on these occasions the dads would turn up to watch the match with huge, professional-looking camcorders to record it. They'd record exciting moments such as when the ball came out of a tightly packed scrum, when there was a slick pass from one player to another, or when we were blessed to witness a tackle worthy of the big league. The excitement, encouragement, and celebration by the parents would also be recorded for future viewing enjoyment.

"If at first you don't succeed, try, try and try again.
At least you'll get fifteen points, twenty-one with conversions."
- Unknown

I was always amused though, that when the boys delighted us with a seamless interception, for example, or displayed excellent side-stepping skills, or there was a try in the making, the camcorders were rendered redundant. Each time one of our fast-paced wingers, with the ball firmly in his grip, would run through the opposition, untouchable and unstoppable, like wind on a breezy day, without fail the dads would move their camcorders aside and watch the moment in real time. The camcorder would be left hanging to the side so that the satisfaction and enjoyment of that special moment could be experienced as it happened. This happened every time. One of the coaches called these moments 'champagne moments.' Later, we'd ask the dads why they did this, saying 'You missed the best bit, you didn't record the best bit. We haven't got the best bit to watch later.' And every time they would respond, 'No, we didn't miss the best bit. We lived the best bit.'

How are you using time?
Use your time wisely, doing things to pursue your dreams. Time is a virtue. It is also a great luxury. When I think of time I am reminded of my big lesson in not taking time for granted. In September 2018 I was due to travel to Lagos, Nigeria to mark the first year anniversary of my dad's passing. I was looking forward to seeing my mum, who had suffered multiple strokes over the previous six years and had become weak and frail since my dad left us. As was customary for us, I'd bought items for her which were difficult to get in Nigeria, mainly medical supplies for her care and comfort.

"Don't become buried treasure. Do it now!"

A week before I was due to travel she became very ill and had to be rushed to hospital. I wanted to change my flight details and leave the UK immediately but she was discharged from hospital the next day. I had work commitments to tie up before my travel date and there would have been cost implications to change my flight. Neither of these would have stopped me, but they were certainly considerations. After discussing with my sister, who was at home with my mum, we decided that it was best for me to continue with my plans. My mum knew my arrival was imminent and was looking forward to seeing me. Two days later, four days before I arrived in Nigeria, my mum passed. I didn't get to see her.

This experience made me begin to look at life differently. I knew I had to act with a sense of urgency. I realised that I had put my dreams on hold. Dreams that had been on hold for so long that they'd lost connection. I knew I had to make the best use of my time. I knew I had to spend time pursuing my passions and positive pursuits. Yet, it took a little more than a year before I developed the courage to do anything about it.

Time is indeed a luxury. How are you using time? How much time do you have left?

"Time is not the main thing.
It is the only thing."
- Miles Davis, 1926 - 1991

Where are you going?

When your life is over, how would you want to be remembered?

Forgive me for asking such a morbid question, but this is the question which gave me the most clarity about my life when I was asked it in July 2020. It gave me a jolt, a flash of reality. My response shocked me more than it did the person who'd asked the question. I hadn't started on any of my life goals. Yes, I am a wife and a mother, but I'm referring to my personal goals. My desires, my dreams. I had long since buried them, believing I had time.

As you begin to write your next chapter, use this question as a prompt: when your life is over, how would you want to be remembered? The destination is the beginning. It is your map; it gives you an idea of where you're going. Think of it like an internal GPS. When you're going somewhere you've never been before, you need a GPS. You input the address of where you're going into the system and it maps a route from where you are to where you want to go. Without a destination address, you'll find yourself driving around and around in circles. This is how it works in life, too. To move on from this page you need to instruct the GPS controlling your life to direct you.

To do this, it makes sense to start at the end: thinking about the legacy you want to leave on earth as the end point. We need a clear picture of what that looks like. Then we can map a path to get there.

"Live your life in such a way
that life doesn't owe you any change."
- Les Brown

15

The first time you think about it, the image may be fuzzy and out of focus. But as you start to write it out, the image becomes clearer and brighter until it is picture perfect.

Let's get some clarity on what that picture looks like. Remember, you are writing it out in your beautiful journal with your magical pen. You can't change the past but you have complete control over the next chapter. You are the author, hero, and editor of this chapter. You get to decide how you want it to be.

What would you write? When your life is over, how would you want to be remembered?

Right now you are in a chapter or season of your life, about to start writing your next chapter. This next chapter is one of enlightenment where you consider what you want in the next act of your life. When you know what that is, it will be a breakthrough moment.

Consider how you want to spend your time in this next chapter and who you'll spend it with. Start and finish the chapter strong. Don't be casual about it because you don't know when it will be over.

"You don't take out the darkness,
you bring in the light."

As I said, this single question gave me the most clarity about my purpose, my mission and my destiny. During my journey (virtual of course) of self-discovery in 2020, I did an exercise which involved writing my own eulogy. This task served as a defibrillator! Once I got over the shock of such a morbid assignment and set about completing it, I realised just how far away I was from any of my goals and dreams. I don't mean to say that I was far from achieving them; I mean that they had even not been factored into my life!

Buried in the deep recesses of my mind were goals and dreams I didn't know I had. It made sense then, why my heart had been trying so hard to get my attention and why I'd felt so unfulfilled. Answering this question forced me to take a long, hard look at my life. I placed a long-distance call to my heart and didn't get off the phone until I got an answer.

Consider the questions in the Spa on the next page and answer them as clearly as possible. Your responses will save you going through life like a rudderless ship, moving without aim or direction. Your dreams are an expression of your vision and your vision is an expression of your purpose.

All the responses you need are inside of you. You need to ask the questions and wait for responses. Tune in to your inner self and pay attention to the responses you get.

*"I had climbed up the corporate ladder but
realised my ladder was against the wrong wall."*

Ask what you need to do to give your life a sense of value. To leave the legacy we want to leave, we need to have done certain things while on earth. We need to get started on those things now.

Be open to doing things that set you on the path to living your dream.

It's your time. Go within and gather the tools you need to step into your life—the life that represents your vision. The life that gives you the opportunity to be the fullest version of you. Seize the moment. Life is uncertain, don't put things off or you'll never get anything done. Become actively engaged in this thing called life.

Live a life that will outlive you—a life through which your impact is felt even when you're gone. As well as leaving a legacy we can also live a legacy. I want to do both, don't you?

"Take control of your life or someone else will."

Spa:
What's your legacy?

Jump ahead to the end of your life:

a) What legacy do you want to leave? What would you want to have done or created?

b) What regrets would you have? What would you wish you'd done more or less of, and why? (Consider the different areas of your life).

c) Imagine that 20 years from now you are winning an award. What would it be in recognition of?

d) What would be your biggest accomplishments and why?

e) What were you doing 5, 10 and 15 years before the end of your life? These are your milestones. Have you started on them yet? If not, why not? Start making plans to get started now. Don't delay! You haven't got the luxury of time, do it now.

f) How do you feel about the end and how would you want to improve it?

"Don't die before you've lived."

Who Do You Think You Are?

As you answer the questions above, you will start to get an idea of where you'd like to see yourself in the future, even beyond your time here. This exercise will also help you to identify gaps between where you are now and where you'd like to go. Let's call that a big roadmap. This roadmap will inform the story you are writing about your future. By the end of this book, you should have identified the detailed map, broken into landmarks.

Now let us add some more details to that roadmap by considering the next question that forms the foundation of your story.

Who are you?

Who are you when no one is watching?

What do you spend your time doing?

What do you talk about?

What are your passions?

What do you love?

What do you dislike?

What is the one thing in the world that you wish you could solve, stop, or create?

Who are you when you're with your friends, just being you, without pressure or fear of judgment?

Which role do you play in your friendship groups?

"You cannot be yourself if you don't know who you are."

No single thing provides a definitive answer to this question. What you want to see are the patterns, any clues which form a trend. They all come together to form the story of who you are.

If we don't know who we are, we cannot possibly know where we're going. We will live from day to day, aimless, like rudderless ships, with no real mission, no goal, no vision.

As you start writing your next chapter, let us ensure that it is a chapter based on *your* dreams, passions, and desires. Have you become an extra in someone else's movie? In this chapter you are the hero, the lead, the reason the movie has been made! Take control of your story and put yourself in it!

As you think about the questions above, ensure you are considering them from your point of view only. It is about what *you* want and no one else. Sometimes we forget what we want because we let other people tell us what we should want. Or we tell ourselves our dream is not possible; it is out of our reach. The brain becomes more committed to the familiar than the unfamiliar, even if the familiar is uncomfortable. It will try to keep you in a familiar discomfort rather than move you to an unfamiliar possibility. It does this because it is designed to keep you safe. Your job is to retrain the brain to say 'Yes' instead of 'No'. Remember that the head (or brain) sees the past and the present and the heart sees the possibilities. These long-buried desires we are conjuring up are coming from your heart. Listen to your heart.

"Don't be an extra in the story of your life."

For a long time I didn't know who I was, I was missing something in my life. I was making a living but I wanted to do more than that. I knew I had more to give. I wanted to do more than make a living; I wanted to make an impact, a real impact. Yes, I'd had great jobs. I realise now that as I moved from one great job to another, I was looking for something. I was looking for something that I thought I would find in the next job. I was looking for the best boss, the best team, the best CEO, the best organisation, the best industry, the best sector, the best anything. What I didn't know was that what I was looking for was me. I was trying to fix an internal challenge with an external solution. So I kept looking, and of course, the more I looked, the less I saw. The answer was everywhere I wasn't looking.

It wasn't until someone said to me, 'If you don't want your boss's job you're in the wrong career'. This was my other wake-up call! It made me sit up and pay attention. It stung. I realised then that I'd carried on doing what I'd always done because it was all I knew how to do.

It was my brain protecting me from possible failure, shame and humiliation. My brain reminded me that I'd tried and failed before. It didn't have a reference of success in business to hang on to, so it rejected ideas of entrepreneurship. That is, until that fateful day in early 2020 when I said, 'Permission granted'.

"If you don't want your boss's job
you're in the wrong career."

For a long time I'd felt I was destined for more. I knew I had untapped potential in me but I was so afraid of not being enough. I suffered from a massive case of imposter syndrome, telling myself I wasn't smart enough, young enough, rich enough, poor enough, experienced enough. Simply, I was afraid I was not enough. So I stayed in my lane. I stayed in the lane I'd become addicted to and shied away from placing any bets on me.

I lacked the courage to bet on me. I didn't believe I had the skills, talents, or gifts to do anything other than what I'd spent the better part of thirty years doing. I know now that I couldn't believe in myself because I didn't know myself. You cannot possibly trust something or someone you do not know. Then life stepped in on me, forcing me to greater heights, to be a blessing. We were created to create. I was breathing but I was not living. I didn't have the courage so life made it impossible for me to stay in my old world. It made it unbearable by putting obstacles which forced me to take a different route. A route to my higher life, my higher calling. A route back to me. I want to encourage you to find a route back to you.

I began the journey of self-discovery, unravelling the layers and cloaks of doubt, the negative and disempowering beliefs which I had adopted over the years. Some of these layers had been placed on me and some I had placed on myself.

"The original is the best, anything else is a copy."

The journey of self-discovery is an internal one and it is indeed a journey, not a destination. The more life experiences you navigate, the more you learn about yourself. As I've said, the answers all lie within you, but you need to be willing to do the work to discover them. I heard a story of someone who described finding himself as looking for a needle in a haystack. He said, 'I was the haystack and I was the needle!'

Don't live your life within the confines of others' expectations of you. There will be clues all around you pointing to who you really are.

In your journal, work through the questions in the Spa section. This is the foundation work; we cannot build on it until the foundation is firm, otherwise anything placed on it will cause it to collapse.

No one can define you better than you. Give yourself permission to define yourself beyond titles, relationships, roles, or circumstances.

"Permission granted!"

Spa:
Know You

Without titles, roles, responsibilities, or circumstances, who are you?

Who were you before the world told you who you were?

Who were you before you lost your dreams?

Who are you when no one is watching?

Think about who you are when you are relaxed. Perhaps when you're out with friends, when your guard is down, and you're just being yourself. When you're not worrying about fitting in, being liked, accepted, or well regarded. When you're not thinking about your responsibilities, cares, and commitments. When you're at your best, just being YOU.

What are the most important things in your life? Your family, your friends, your home, your work? These give your life value and meaning.

What are your passions and dreams? Think about the activities that excite and thrill you.

Consider your values, beliefs, and principles. What qualities do you possess? What do you represent?

If you were guaranteed 100% success, what would you do?

What voices are you hearing? What are they saying?

What do you need to give yourself permission to do?

What is holding you back?

"Create a bucket list of things that you have always
wanted to do, and then get them out of the bucket!"

\- Les Brown

What Are Your Superpowers?

You have natural talents and abilities, which I will collectively refer to as superpowers. You use your superpowers so naturally and effortlessly, you may not even realise when or how you do so. They are unique to you and they identify you to the world, just like your fingerprint or DNA. You do not need to learn them, and you cannot stop doing them. They are who you are.

Your superpowers are the things that people think of when they think of you and when an example is sought to illustrate that talent, your name is mentioned.

If you don't already know what your superpowers are, take some time to identify them. Recognising your superpowers is empowering and confidence-boosting. Also, when you use them, you are being authentic and true to yourself.

Your superpowers work best with the rest of you, making you the whole person you are. Adopting another persona is like the proverbial 'fitting a round peg in a square hole.' It wouldn't fit because they were not designed to go together! Your superpowers work best for you, with you, and by you. Find them and flaunt them!

"Use what you've got."

Often, we dismiss and disregard our superpowers. When we do, we diminish our gifts and deny ourselves the opportunity to use them to our advantage. A melodic voice, an engaging smile, the ability to say kind words, or a generous spirit are all superpowers and everybody should own their unique superpowers. For example, having a beautiful smile will give you a positive countenance that will make people feel comfortable around you. What are your superpowers?

For a long time I didn't think I had any superpowers because I thought they had to be something tangible, something I could make or create and present to people. I thought they had to be something to do with cooking, baking, or art, for example, because I recognised only these as the expressions of creativity. While I can cook and bake quite well, I have no desire to do either of these things every day for the rest of my life. As for art, I struggle to draw a straight line with a ruler! My husband, on the other hand, is a natural artist. As an architect, art is one of his many special gifts.

It wasn't until 2020 that I realised, thanks to a friend, that something I had been overlooking for a long time, a very long time, is one of my biggest superpowers. I'd always thought it was me just doing me. Well, it was, and that is why we often take our superpowers for granted. My superpower is the ability to be a source of truth.

We all have superpowers. Find yours and serve them to the world.

I am able to help people easily clear the weeds from the path so they can navigate a way through. This is often delivered with a healthy dose of humour, which is not always appreciated!

When you use your superpowers you are adding value to another person's life. When you add value to another person, you add value to yourself. In the words of Les Brown, 'Love, hope, and inspiration are like perfume. You can't get some on others without getting some on yourself'.

As women, we often find it difficult to own our greatness, believing it to be vanity. We don't want to attract attention and so we become highly skilled at deflecting praise or compliments. Please release this habit. Own your superpower. It is your special gift and it'd be rude not to flaunt it.

So, what are your superpowers? Recognise them and enjoy serving them to the world.

"You have something special.
Whether you realise it or not,
the world is a better place because you are here."

Spa:
You have them, recognise them!

What do strangers immediately notice when they first meet you?

Is it your sense of humour, your ability to say calming words?

Is it your engaging or disarming smile?

Is it your warmth, kindness, empathy, generosity, confidence, self-awareness, compassion, or vibrance? You may be surprised to find that you have more than one superpower!

Your superpowers will be the things that people are reminded of when they hear your name. These qualities are associated with you and you with them.

Identifying your superpowers can be empowering.

Identify yours and flaunt them!

Spend time doing the things that you love and which bring you joy.

"Say 'yes' to your superpowers."

To be the best version of yourself, you must first love yourself.

To love yourself, you must first know yourself.

Sweet is my smile,

unique is my style.

I'm perfect in my
imperfections,

happy in my pain.

Strong in my weaknesses
and

beautiful in my own way.

I Am Me!

- Unknown

The Awakening

I peered out of the small window in the small office on the thirteenth floor, wondering if it was raining. I couldn't tell. It was 5:28 p.m. on January 29, 2020, a cold, dark evening in London. My eyes stared into the dark skies, tired from the ridiculously late nights I'd been working for the past few weeks. I was exhausted, physically and mentally, but didn't see any hope of an end in sight on the three major deliverables I was in charge of. I'd been working 16 to 18 hour days for the previous few weeks, often up until four or five in the morning, and on one occasion I remember working throughout the night.

'Shall I dial-in now?' my team member said, bringing me back to reality. 'Yes, it's time', I said, 'let's do this.' I felt some trepidation and said a silent prayer for wisdom, tact, and sound judgement as she punched the Skype number into the spider phone attached to the desk. I leaned over to move the phone closer to her so she wouldn't have to stretch so far, but it was attached to the desk. I'd always wondered why the phones in some offices were attached to the desks but not in others. I looked at my watch and said to myself, 'Well, here goes. How do I let him know that I'm just the middle-person, working hard to progress this, but there is a process which I need to work through, including getting little-available market data, as part of the supporting information required for this request to be fully considered?'

"Your challenges are stepping
stones to greater success."

'How do I let him know that the blockage was not from me? What can I do to progress this to its conclusion? Not just for him but for me too, so I can get some sleep. How will this play out?' He was a senior leader, waiting for an update on a business case request. A request which had robbed me of many hours of sleep.

The meeting started pleasantly enough with 6 individuals present. Then it was time for me to provide my update. I delivered an honest update. Perhaps that was my error. I didn't coat it in 'business speak'. We were still working on it and needed more time to complete the due diligence process and for us to gather what little external market data was available. Silence. Then out it came, the frustration and anger as the senior leader realised that this was not what he was expecting to hear. He ranted and raved, his voice getting louder with each sentence. His angry roar boomed through the phone, causing the small room to vibrate. I tried to move the phone away from me, he was shouting so loud I could hear his voice inside my own head. But the phone didn't move, it was attached to the desk.

Beads of sweat ran down my face and my pulse quickened. My mouth opened but no words came out. This was a good thing because I wouldn't have trusted what would have come out. As he went on, I could feel myself about to explode. The physical and mental strain of the previous few weeks was not helping. My head was pounding, throbbing like it was being hit against a wall.

"Stop looking for light at the end of the tunnel.
You are the light. Shine."
- Fela Durotoye

Finally, he stopped. My mouth opened once again. Suddenly, a silent calm came over me. My mouth closed; my head was empty of any thoughts. My heart was at peace. I was still, deadly still. I looked around the room. I looked at the spider phone sitting silently in front of me, not a sound coming through it. Well, apart from the heavy breathing that had replaced the roar. He was waiting for a response. I looked outside. I still couldn't tell if it was raining.

Through the brain fog I was experiencing, I was able to see clearly, like scales had been removed from my eyes. Quietly, very quietly, I said, 'Not today.' No words came out of my mouth. The meeting ended, though I don't remember any more of it. I knew it was time. As I left the building, I knew it was time for me to jump and grow my wings on the way down. Outside, in the cold January air, I tightened my coat around me. I didn't look back. Oh, it wasn't raining.

The next morning I asked myself, 'Now what?' What is your 'Now what?' What are you going through in life right now that is making you question what is next for you? Life is built on disruption, transformation, and doing new things to catch up and close the gap—events that leave us feeling broken, lost, and stuck. I'm here to tell you that you're not broken; you don't need to be fixed. And you're not lost, though you may have become disconnected from your soul, your power, your source. Recognising this disconnection is the first step to reconnection. Now, let's get you connected. This time, with you fully in control.

"I am enough."

Often, as we journey through life, we consciously or subconsciously adopt cloaks and personas to adapt to our external circumstances. We become different versions of ourselves, and as time goes by, we lose sight of who we really are. We drift along aimlessly, living a misplaced life, wearing unwanted labels and other people's expectations of us. This inevitably leads to frustration because we are not being our true selves.

When you lose connection with yourself, your natural spark, your essence, and your uniqueness are also lost. You feel trapped. You don't know where you are or how you got there, but you know you do not belong there.

To regain control of our lives, we need to remove these cloaks and labels, unburden ourselves of the expectations of others, and become our authentic selves again. This means you are stepping out of line, but in doing so, you're stepping back into the right line, the line you were in before you became someone else. Discover your greatness and wear it with the pride it deserves. You have something special in you, you were born for something. Get quiet and reconnect with yourself.

I had certainly lost connection with myself. I'd been drifting along in life, knowing that there was something missing but unaware of where I lost it or what it looked like. I am grateful for this January meeting because it gave me the much-needed wake-up call to rediscover myself.

"Look back and thank God, look ahead and praise God, look around and serve God, look within and seek God."

Aside from a four-year stint as a business owner between 2000 and 2004, I'd worked in the corporate world for the last three decades. I had a great career in Human Resources at some of the most recognisable global corporate organisations. I thought I was doing all right because I was doing all right but increasingly, I felt a pull, a void in my heart, a voice in my head, an inner yearning for more. Sometimes things are going so well on the outside but inside we are broken. Sometimes we hold ourselves back from operating in our fullness. I knew there was more, something was missing, but I didn't know what it was. I didn't have the courage to find out what it was. I didn't give myself permission. I couldn't muster up the courage.

I had suffered a business failure in 2004 which had left me broke and broken. Some of the shame, humiliation, fear, and pain from that devastating experience was still bleeding into my life, holding me hostage and leaving me stuck.

I knew I could do more. I wanted to create my own future. I wanted to be reconnected with my dreams, to see the possibilities in my life, but I was afraid to give myself a chance. I didn't believe I had anything to offer. I saw only my failures, my weaknesses, my limitations, and my past mistakes. I saw every flaw that I have and some which I don't have.

"The difference you're looking for is in your hands."

On that fateful January evening, in an office in London's Southbank, the price that I was paying to stay in my old world became higher than the price I was afraid to pay if I left. That was the day I said, 'Permission granted.'

What voice are you hearing in your head and in your heart, and what is it saying? It may start softly and subtly. It may be a yearning. It's coming from your heart. Your heart knows your dreams and desires, and it is trying to communicate with you. If you ignore it, it'll only get louder and louder until it becomes deafening. Listen to it, listen to your heart.

Give yourself permission to get to a place where you can stand in our own power and greatness. You have so much power inside of you, waiting for you to give yourself permission to unleash your greatness to the world.

If somebody wants 'A' to happen,
yet they prepare for 'B',
They will always get 'B'.
Prepare for 'A'.
Believe, and prepare for 'A'.

CHAPTER TWO

Be You

———

"Mind is the master power that moulds and makes.
He thinks in secret and it comes to pass;
environment is but his looking-glass."
- James Allen, 1864 - 1912, As A Man Thinketh

State of Mind

You attract what your mind focuses on

Your attention on a subject is your invitation. We have all experienced situations where we think of someone, and within a few minutes we get a call or message from that person. You think of something, and as if by magic, it appears or happens, sometimes instantly.

The mind is an immensely powerful tool and we attract into our lives whatever we focus on. Your mind does what it thinks you want based on your thoughts, so it is your job to tell it what you want by thinking the right thoughts.

It's all in your mind

We literally think our lives into being by the thoughts we hold in our minds. We come into the world with a phenomenal mind, but as we journey through life, we adopt negative, limiting beliefs through the people and circumstances we experience.

Sometimes, our thoughts tell us we are not good enough by giving us a daily inventory of our flaws, weaknesses, past mistakes, and negative experiences. This becomes our default way of thinking. We start to believe it, and since we get more of what we think about, it becomes a self-fulfilling prophecy. Our thoughts become our reality and our thoughts become things.

"No one rises to low expectations."

If you think you are clumsy, you will notice every action of yours that confirms that view. The more actions you notice, the more convinced you become.

When you have a low expectation of yourself or of other people, you treat them in a certain way. It shows in the way you look at them, how you talk to them, and the tools, time, energy, and support you make available for them. When someone is told they're no good and will not amount to much, they might accept this as true. We respond to who we're told we are and to other people's expectations of us. No one should be labelled. Labels belong on jars. Reject any labels! Reject any labels on yourself or anyone you know.

What do you see?

Some people never have anything positive to say. They complain about everything: the weather, their job, their home, their partner, their children, politics, the government, etc. It is no surprise that they never see anything to be positive about. What you feed your focus expands. If complaining and negativity is the default state of your being, your mind obliges. So, the cycle of having more negative experiences is perpetuated. And on and on it goes.

What have you allowed your mind to focus on? What negative words have you repeatedly told yourself? What negative words have you been told?

"Someone else's opinion of you does not have to become your reality."
- Mike Williams

What thoughts are holding you back from reaching for your goals and dreams? If you don't believe in yourself, no one else will.

Do an assessment of the thoughts which you may have unconsciously allowed into your beliefs. Which of these do you still believe that may be affecting how you show up in life?

It is time for a change

Be intentional about what you see, believe, and focus on. Fill your mind with positive reading and affirmations daily. One way to do this is to read at least 30 minutes of positive and uplifting words every day. This trains the mind by feeding it with positive information. You cannot always filter your thoughts, but you can control which thoughts you focus on. And because what you feed your focus expands, feed it with positive words.

Beliefs

Beliefs are powerful. From our beliefs we construct a narrative about ourselves, others, and the world. They are the foundation of our self-image and they direct the mind. If we do not believe we are worthy or deserving, the mind will accept that to be true and will destroy any contrary actions. Without dismantling our current limiting belief system, we cannot expect to be empowered to step into our greatness. We need to challenge the beliefs which do not support who we really are and who we want to be. Unpack your current belief system and let go of any beliefs that do not represent the new you.

"What other people think of you is none of your business."
- Unknown

Ignite a spirit of 'I am enough! I can do this'. This will empower you to take control of your life and take the first step to start writing the next chapter.

How we live our lives is a result of the story we believe about ourselves. Tell yourself a better story. Write the script the way you want it to go. Live your life from a place of power, knowing that what you have been through will not define you. Change your mindset and expand your vision by creating a new set of beliefs which corresponds to the new you.

Here are a few examples of negative, limiting beliefs:
- Money is evil. Wealthy people are evil
- The world is dangerous
- Life is hard
- People who look like me do not achieve success

To achieve a personal breakthrough, we must work on our belief system, which is similar to upgrading an operating system. It is the framework on which our internal thoughts, actions, and habits are based. The journey toward empowerment begins with installing a new belief system in your mind. Think about what you want to experience in your life and replace the old negativity with new, positive, and uplifting possibilities. It is a mind reprogramming process, like mind surgery. Which of your beliefs are serving you and which do you need to offload?

"Whether you think you can or think you can't, you're right."
- Henry Ford, 1863 - 1947

I am reminded of a day when I drove into a petrol station to fill up my car. I must have been distracted because when I went into the shop to pay and the attendant asked which pump I had used, my mind went blank. He then pointed to my car and said, 'Are you the Lexus RX450H with £68 diesel? 'Well, yes but no. I'm the Lexus RX450H but with £68 petrol, not diesel'.

He looked at the screen in front of him, looked outside in the direction of my car and very dryly, said, 'Well, love, you've just filled up your petrol tank with diesel'. His calm, dry tone suggested that perhaps this was a familiar occurrence to him. In his line of work I guess we can call it an occupational hazard.

Utter disbelief. Surely, he was wrong. I went outside to check and yes, there it was. The value of the fuel I'd pumped in my car was firmly showing against 'Diesel'. My car could not be driven and I called the AA, a vehicle emergency rescue service. When the AA guy arrived (this seems to be the generic term used by many people when they're referring to the car rescue engineer – 'the AA guy') he shook his head when I told him what I'd done. 'Is this a big problem?' I asked. 'Not a big problem', he said, 'but a big job'. I learned that my car would need to be towed to a workshop for its tank to be completely drained and cleaned before being filled with the gas that it was built to run on. It is the same with the mind.

"The biggest wall you have to climb is the one you build in your mind."

When we fill our minds with negative, fearful, limiting beliefs, we must eliminate these beliefs before we can be the best versions of ourselves.

We must believe that we are worthy, that we have value, and that we have the power to be all that we were created to be. Start by holding a mental picture of yourself the way you'd like to be. Then replace the old thought patterns by refilling the mind with uplifting thoughts of positivity, courage, and expectation. Ensure that these new beliefs align with who you want to be and how you see yourself from now on.

Say affirmations and crowd your mind with empowering words of hope, courage, and faith. What negative beliefs have you adopted? What are you saying to yourself about yourself? The beliefs that brought you to where you are today cannot take you where you want to go.

As I stepped up my life to reinvent myself, I drew courage and inspiration from a few books. Six of these books became my constant companions and they changed my life in 2020. They inspired me to let go of my fears and to give myself permission to live my life with no regrets. They remain my 'go-to' even now for words of wisdom, inspiration, and a prescription for living a more fulfilled life. I'd like to share with you the two which impacted me immeasurably.

"When you change the way you look at things,
the things you look at change."
- Wayne Dyer

The first is *You've Got To Be Hungry* by Les Brown. This book is simple to read yet packed with powerful inspiration and great wisdom. In this book, Les Brown, one of the greatest motivational speakers in the world, shares the story of his life.

He says he has two mothers. One gave him life but could not raise him or his twin brother, so she adopted him out to his other mother, who gave him love. He was told at school at a young age that he was 'educable mentally retarded'. This is not a term I am familiar with—suffice it to say that he was considered dumb. The other kids referred to him as DT. This stands for Dumb Twin. Even Les accepted this as fact.

One day he was standing at the back of a class waiting for a friend, and the teacher asked him to come up and answer a question. Les looked around, wondering who the teacher was referring to. The teacher said, 'You, yes, you. Come up here and answer the question.'

The other kids started to laugh and Les said, 'I can't.' The teacher asked, 'Why not?' The kids said, 'He's DT', to which the teacher responded, 'What's DT?' 'Dumb twin', they said, 'He's the dumb twin. He's not Wesley, he's Leslie, he's the dumb twin.'

Les said to his teacher, 'That's right, Sir, I'm DT, I'm the dumb twin. I can't answer the question.' The teacher then said, 'Who told you that? Never let someone else's opinion of you become your reality.'

"What you see in your life is first conceived in your mind."

This teacher went on to become Les Brown's mentor and set him up on the road to greatness. Les Brown, who has spoken to and motivated people around the world, including an 80,000-person crowd at the Georgia Dome, was written off as educable mentally retarded.

It was this book which helped me find my voice. After reading it, I thought to myself, 'I want to do this. This is me, this is home. I'm going to do this.' There's barely a page in the book which doesn't have a tip, a lesson, a message to use to live a more fulfilled life. Its simplicity adds to its usability and adoptability. I love it. I have tried, without

46

success, to decide whether it's my book of the year. It may well be, but this position is closely followed by the next book I'm including here.

The second book is *Jump* by Steve Harvey. In this book, Steve shares principles from his life journey, thoughts on how we can take a leap and jump towards our hopes and dreams. This book resonated strongly with me because Steve talks about people who are doing jobs they don't like, ignoring their dreams while their God-given gifts lie unused and wasting away. Steve uses stories of his own failures, unfortunate moments, such as the infamous Miss Universe pageant saga when an incorrect winner's name was read out, to a period when he lived from his car, to explain his life principles. At the heart of this book is Steve's principle of having the faith to take a leap and elevate his life. Steve says that if God did it for him, He will do it for everyone; we just need to jump.

"You are more than your circumstances."

The other books which most inspired me in my reinvention journey are *The Power of Positive Thinking* by Norman Vincent Peale, *In Pursuit of Purpose* by Myles Munroe, *Think And Grow Rich* by Napoleon Hill, and *As A Man Thinketh* by James Allen.

As you step towards the new you, the new life you want for yourself, you will encounter obstacles, challenges, and defeats. You will need to have a reference point, an anchor on which you can draw faith. These are the places you go to give you courage and inspiration to carry on. Find things that stimulate you, that empower you, that require you to constantly aim to be a better version of yourself today than you were yesterday. It is necessary to aim for the next level, the next step. As well as surrounding yourself with people who want you to be better, people who help you elevate yourself and raise your personal bar, you also need to learn from people within the field of what you want to do, either directly or indirectly. Keep learning, keep growing, and keep aiming for more. Always be a student of life.

How you see your life, your situation, and your circumstances and what you think you cannot control or change is determined by your point of view. Create a new perspective, a new point of view, by changing your beliefs, thoughts, and words about yourself. Tell yourself a different story.

"Accept responsibility for your life.
Know that it is you who will get you where
you want to go, no one else."

Create a new belief system
Beliefs are personal to everyone, so create an empowering belief system based on your life, your current beliefs, and the new you. Here are some beliefs that resonate with me:

1. Everything that I am seeking is also seeking me.
2. I am more powerful than I know; I can do everything I want.
3. I believe I will always take the right turn in the road.
4. I will make use of any opportunity granted to me.
5. There is always a way.
6. I forgive everyone, including myself.
7. I already have everything that I need.

8. I take 100% responsibility for my future. No one is in charge of me. I have the power to control my life.

9. My happiness, peace, and joy are my responsibility.

10. I dream big and deserve all that is good in my life.

11. I understand my potential. I can be anything that I want.

12. My past does not define my future.

13. Life is exciting, fun, and satisfying.

14. There is good in the world.

15. I trust my journey and the process of my life.

16. I am in control of my destiny.

17. Everything that I experience happens for me and not to me.

18. As I start to walk on the way, the way appears.

19. Everything I want is making its way to me.

20. I love life and life loves me.

"Change your attitude of how you see yourself,
how you define yourself, how you treat yourself,
and how you allow others to treat you."

Take action

Your life will not magically change by just altering your thoughts. You will need to reinforce it with the required follow-up action. However, if your thoughts and beliefs are not in alignment with the life you want to create, they will not accept it. Remove your mind from the 'scene of the crime' and back this up by providing the right emotional space in which to create the new you.

Saying positive affirmations to yourself in front of the mirror everyday is a powerful way to begin to change your belief system. Our mind, our thoughts, and our beliefs are the writers, the editors, the producers, the directors, and the actors of our life story. When you change them, you get a new script and a different set of life outcomes.

That's life,
some days are smooth like a flat paved road,
other days seem all uphill.
Some days you'll think that life stood still,
But that's life, you can live it if you will.

Spa:
Get unstuck

To get unstuck, you must destroy your negative beliefs.

What beliefs are preventing you from reaching your goals and dreams? It is time to replace them with ones that will serve you better and represent the life you want.

Challenge yourself by questioning your beliefs. Have they always been true? Sometimes, when we change our perspective, we realise how narrow our previous beliefs were.

Create a new belief system around your aspirations and inspirations. Replace your negative, limiting beliefs with positive, empowering ones. Include all areas of your life in your new belief system: your home, your relationships, your health, your career.

What are you telling yourself about you?

Positive affirmations are a powerful way of changing our belief system. Use the affirmations in this book, adding any of your favourite ones.

"Change your mind to change your life."

Like attracts like

So, now we know that our thoughts frame our minds. We also know that the more focus and attention we give a thought, the bigger it gets and the more we attract and realise it into our lives. So, if you say things like, 'I'm a failure', 'I'm lazy', 'I'm so broke', your mind accepts this as true and it becomes your reality.

When things are going well, it is easy to believe in yourself and believe life is good. However, when things aren't going so well, when you are experiencing challenges or embracing new experiences, it is necessary to have faith and adopt strong, positive beliefs. While it may be difficult, it is necessary and possible. Ultimately, you need to believe in the unseen. As the saying goes, 'don't believe everything you think.'

Those voices in your head

Beliefs carry powerful emotions, which influence our actions. We self-sabotage by thinking we are not worthy, not deserving. We fixate on our mistakes, failures, circumstances, and weaknesses. We even showcase to ourselves every physical, emotional, or intellectual flaw we have, including some we did not realise we had. 'But my bank account tells me I'm poor', 'I was told I was ugly when I was a child', 'I don't fit in', 'I'm not the right colour', 'I'm over/underweight', and the list goes on and on.

"Believe that everything is possible!"

Do not label or disqualify yourself from life or allow people or circumstances to make you feel unworthy. A negative self-image and limiting beliefs lead to feelings such as fear, insecurity, disempowerment, depression, and unworthiness.

The image below illustrates how our beliefs affect what we see in our lives. Your beliefs become your thoughts. These thoughts become your default habits, which become your actions, and your actions become your reality. Do you want to live in a way that showcases your negative thoughts, or your empowering ones?

"For as he thinketh in his heart, so is he."
- Holy Bible, KJV, Proverbs 23:7

There are stories of wealthy people who lose all their money and make it back again. Their fundamental belief system matches wealth creation. Is it possible, then, that this might also explain why some people get rich quickly, by winning the lottery for example, and lose it in a short space of time? They do not believe they are wealthy, so their thoughts, habits, and actions do not support their new wealth. Similarly, it is possibly the same reason some people lose weight and within a short time, put it back on again. To achieve a different outcome we must generate positive and empowering thoughts that support the new version of ourselves.

Breakthroughs happen when we believe. Open your heart to the possibility. If you do not yet believe you can have a new life, instead of telling yourself you can't have it, just keep an open mind. Leave the door of possibility open. Start with 'it's possible.' Let go of things in your life that are not serving you and create a new belief system, one that spurs you to positive decisions and actions that empower you to change. Your life experiences are the result of your focus and beliefs. The key to positive life experiences is to replace the limiting beliefs of fear, rejection, and unworthiness with new beliefs. Your level of belief in yourself inevitably manifests in your life, and what you create inside of you becomes your reality outside of you.

"If you want something you've never had, you must be willing to do something you've never done before."
- Thomas Jefferson

Spa:
Thoughts become things

What do you believe about yourself?

Who do you see when you look in the mirror?

Train your mind to think positively. Remember that your mind is the window to your life and what you see in your mind is a prelude to what you will see in your life.

Write out a new belief list that describes how you want to see yourself and who you are becoming. Include all areas of your life including love, health, family, relationships, career, money, and so on.

---

*"Your job is to tell your mind
what you want."*

Mind Your Language

How do you speak to yourself? We sometimes speak negatively to and about ourselves, in ways that would be considered unacceptable to speak to anyone else. Are you harsh and critical with yourself, perhaps even abusive? 'Ugh, I'm so clumsy', 'Look what I've just done', 'How silly!', 'I don't believe I've just done that again, look how foolish I am!', 'Look at me, I never have any luck', 'Get a grip!' and so on.

Pay attention to your internal dialogue; you may be surprised at your language and tone. Words have power and they carry meaning. They have profound powers of suggestion and when we say these words to ourselves, our minds comply, believing that that is what we want. It then gives us similar circumstances to match what it believes are instructions from us. We begin to 'feel' the words we say and then we experience more circumstances to match.

It is necessary to speak kindly to yourself and not in a negative, self-sabotaging way. When you think these thoughts and are about to say something, get in the habit of catching yourself and ask, 'Do I really think that? Do I really mean to call myself these words? Do I really feel I am clumsy, stupid, etc.?'

When you speak to yourself, ask yourself if what you are saying is something you would say to someone you love if they were in a similar situation.

"What you speak about, you bring about."

Would you say to a friend, 'Look at you, you're so clumsy, you're so stupid'? If you wouldn't do it to someone else, why would you do it to yourself?

This is one of my challenge areas. I used to constantly berate myself for making even the tiniest errors, which I viewed as evidence of my ineptitude. It is still an area of work in progress for me. Now I have started to catch myself just as the thought pops into my head and I celebrate myself each time. Oh, don't forget to celebrate your small victories!

Those words you say

Words can be immensely powerful. Words spoken with power, feelings, and conviction materialise faster. The right words can provide inspiration, motivation, and encouragement to break free from a damaging situation. Negative words arise from fear, rejection, and unworthiness, which can fuel a state of depression and disempowerment.

No labels

Be mindful of your words and pay attention to your self-talk. A situation labelled as 'bad' has no option but to be so, because your mind accepts the description and closes the door to possibilities. Also, because you are thinking 'bad', your thinking will attract more experiences of the same.

Positive words open the door to possibilities and a different perspective. Life is dynamic; people, circumstances, and situations evolve, so it is wise to be open-minded to allow the possibility of change or growth.

"Did you mean to say that?"

To create a new life after many years of using self-deprecating words, you have to change your negative thoughts and words about yourself. Be mindful of what you say to yourself, only saying things to yourself about yourself that you believe to be true or wish to be true.

Be kind to yourself; let your self-talk mirror the way you would speak to someone you love. You are loving, lovable, and deserving. Say kind words to yourself.

Here is a list of words I intentionally refrain from using casually. I am certain you can add to the list., Feel free to do so.

Rejection – *use* **Redirection**

In many cases, hindsight teaches us that what we originally thought was a rejection was actually a God-sent redirection. A 'rejection' is a redirection from the universe to open yourself up to new opportunities and new possibilities in your life.

Problem – *use* **Challenge**

A challenge is an opportunity for God to reveal himself. See the blessing and know that all will be well.

Regret – *use* **Recalibration**

Do not regret your past. The experiences we gain in life shape and mould us in preparation for our future. Learn the lessons from the experiences and move forward.

"What you say matters."

Failure – *use* **Experience**

We don't fail; we learn, we gain valuable experiences and we evolve. When asked how it felt to fail 1,000 times, Thomas Edison said, 'I did not fail, I found 999 ways that did not work.'

To – *use* **For**

Things do not happen to you, they happen for you. Whatever may have happened is just an episode or an interruption in your life. It is not the end. Learn from the episode and identify the opportunity.

Lose – *use* **Release**

When we say we lose something we instinctively look for ways to find it or replace it. To let go of something, we release it or give it up. So, we do not lose weight, we release or let go of weight. If you don't want it back, let it go!

"Words are powerful, choose them wisely."

Spa

Words have meaning and power.

Words are creative, choose them wisely.

Sometimes all you need is a change of perspective to see things differently.

Don't label people, circumstances, or situations as 'good' or bad'. Things sometimes unfold vastly differently from how they first appeared.

What you say matters.

What you speak about, you bring about.

"There are blessings in closed doors."

Passion, Power, Purpose, and Possibilities

Purpose: *the reason, intention, or objective for which something is done or created, or for which something exists.*

Why are you here?

Now that you know who you are, the next question is, why? Why were you created? What are you meant to do with your life?

You are not here by accident; you were created for a bigger purpose. What is that purpose? If your life were a house, your purpose would be the foundation.

Everyone was born with a gift, a special gift that is connected to our passions, our dreams, our desires. We were created to have value and to add value. When we live a life of purpose, we are in full alignment with our natural selves. We can live a full life, using our skills, talents, and gifts to their full potential. When we feel stuck, when we feel unfulfilled, when we feel lost or trapped, it is often due to the fact that we're not in true alignment with our purpose.

Discovering your purpose is one of your most important gifts to self-actualisation. You were born to do more than work and die. Your job is to discover your purpose and serve it to the world.

"The two most important days in our life are the day we were born
and the day we find out why we were born."
- Mark Twain, 1835 – 1910

Like a compass, your purpose guides you. Until you discover it, your life can feel like a rudderless ship, going around in circles with no aim or direction. It pulls and calls you, but, caught up in life's distractions, you may not hear or recognise it, so you remain adrift.

Knowing your purpose is a major step to living a conscious life. Your purpose awakens goals and dreams; it presents opportunities, giving you focus, meaning, and energy. It is like getting the master key to a life of fulfillment, authenticity, and identity.

I remember one time when my girlfriend and I shared a rented apartment and needed to unscrew a cap or something. We looked around the apartment, searching for a screwdriver. We didn't have one so we finally gave up and decided to use a kitchen knife instead. The kitchen knife got the job done but it got damaged in the process and took a lot longer than a screwdriver would have. It did not do the job in the same way as the screwdriver because what we used it for was not its intended use.

It is the same with us. We may be able to do well enough if we apply ourselves to pursuits other than those for which we were created, but this is a recipe for unfulfillment, failure, and frustration, which are not enjoyable experiences. When we apply ourselves to our intended purpose, we are elegant, fulfilled, and satisfied. It may not always be easy but it feels natural and empowering and propels us to pursue our passions.

"Purpose leaves clues."

It is said that you should not ask about the meaning of life, you should ask about the meaning of your life. Like a car, we are all born with an owner's manual. Our manual describes our intended purpose. The way to discover that purpose is to read the manual. To find your manual, look within you, be introspective. The answers are not outside of you, they never are. The answers are within you. Take time to listen to your heart. Listen to the voice of your spirit. Find somewhere quiet and get in touch with your inner self by listening intently and recording what you hear. Techniques such as journaling and scripting are effective tools for accessing your inner self and are discussed later in *The Inner Sanctuary*.

When you are out of alignment with who you really are, listen to your heart, listen to your dreams. Where do your dreams come from? They come from your heart.

Your passions and dreams lead to your purpose and to your 'unstuckness'. Your purpose gives you power, and when you have power you see possibilities. When you listen to your heart, it tells you what you really want. Your heart knows the possibilities of your life; it knows the life you want to live and can direct you. You just need to tune in to it and listen.

It is not lost

You do not need to find your purpose because it cannot be lost. You only need to discover, recognise, or realise it. It does not need to be learned, but, like a diamond, it can be refined.

"You are phenomenal. Be phenomenal."

Find the courage

It takes courage to live a purposeful life, especially if it goes against others' expectations of you. On the other hand, a life without purpose results in frustration, unfulfillment, and discontentment. Your talents, abilities, gifts, circumstances, failures, and defeats are part of your journey in life, equipping you for your purpose. They are connected, forming the experiences and resources which help you fulfill your purpose and destiny. Embrace the journey of discovering your purpose. It is exciting, rewarding, fulfilling, and empowering.

Your heart is connected to your purpose. It is powerful; it knows why you are here, it knows your past, present, and future. That's why you feel frustrated and unfulfilled when you are out of alignment with your purpose. These feelings are coming from your heart. Your heart is telling you that you are not doing what you are supposed to be doing, you aren't listening to it.

'What am I meant to do with my life?' This is a question I asked myself for a long time. I looked everywhere for my purpose, like it was lost. I used to walk around asking, 'Where's my purpose? Where's my purpose? Is it here? Is it there?' I looked everywhere around me and the more I looked, the less I saw.

"Gifts cannot be taught, they are freely given.
Birds are not taught to fly or fish to swim."

64

In the words of Les Brown, 'You cannot read the label when you're locked inside the box', and you 'cannot see the picture when you're stuck inside the frame.'

Purpose, as they say, leaves clues. I moved to the UK from Nigeria in 1990. Actually, I came on holiday, met my husband, fell in love, and stayed in the UK, but that's a story for another book. When I came to the UK, I had no intention of remaining here and brought two books with me for comfort. One is the Holy Bible, which was a gift from my parents, and the other is a book called, *Bring Out The Magic In Your Mind*. This book by Al Koran teaches about the mind, belief, and using the tools within you to create the life you desire. It has gone everywhere with me since I first got my hands on it at the age of 14 or 15. I have never been too far away from it and I've read it many times over. It has provided me with much hope, inspiration, and encouragement since I first read it.

When I finally decided to pay attention to the void in my heart and listen to the voice in my head, it was no surprise that this book led a path to the work of my dreams. Who knew? For many years I thought I was unambitious, in spite of any perceived professional success. I was surrounded by well-accomplished people and measured against many, my professional ambitions dimmed in comparison.

"Your passion gives you permission to pursue your purpose."

I had great roles and had the opportunity to work with extremely smart individuals in global, recognisable corporate organisations. I was fortunate to travel widely, both personally and professionally, and expand my skills, knowledge, and experience. For this I will always be grateful. These opportunities led me to where I am today, as I am a cumulation of all my previous experiences. I always 'knew' there was more. I had no desire to rise to the top of any of the organisations at which I worked. I knew I was able to do more, I knew I wanted more, but I didn't know what it was. I wondered what was wrong with me. Now I know that it was my heart calling me towards my dreams, towards my purpose. I know now that I was measuring my accomplishments against another person's ruler. What a waste! My head saw my past and present, with all my failures, weaknesses and limitations. My heart saw my passion, purpose, power, and possibilities.

A few weeks ago I came across an old journal of mine from 2010. On the third page is a list of my dream jobs. I was shocked to find on the list Life Coach and Motivational Speaker! I did not realise that I'd had these dreams since 2010, but it really should not have been a surprise, considering that I'd taken *Bring Out The Magic In Your Mind* everywhere I went since 1980! Purpose indeed, leaves clues. In the words of Rumi, 'Whatever you are seeking is also seeking you.'

"A man's gift maketh room for him..."
- Holy Bible, KJV, Proverbs 18:16

I realised that what I'd been searching for for so many years had been inside of me the whole time, trying to be heard—but of course, I was totally oblivious to this. I've finally discovered my purpose. The purpose that I was already living. The purpose that is my passion. The purpose that has been driving my life, inspiring women to be the best they can be. To redefine themselves and not allow themselves to be defined by their relationships, titles, or circumstances. To have an expanded vision of themselves. It is the best decision I ever made. But it wasn't easy, it was challenging. I had to overcome my past failures and my past mistakes. I also had to overcome myself. I had to get out of my own way. I had to develop the courage to bet on myself and step into my purpose.

Your purpose is your gift. You were created with a gift, equipped for your gift, and resourced to deliver your gift. When you use your gift you increase your value and you are operating in your fullness. When you first take the leap to walk in your purpose, it can feel like turbulence in an aeroplane. When you get on a plane, before take-off, they tell you to fasten your seatbelt. Why? Because you are going to experience some turbulence before you reach a comfortable cruising altitude. Expect some turbulence when you take the first few steps. You've been out of alignment with your purpose for such a long time, so it will take a little while for you to settle down and reach a comfortable cruising altitude. It is worth it though, for a lifetime of fulfillment and purpose. It is an awakening, it is empowering, and you look forward to each day with great joy, anticipation, and desire.

"Experiment until you find the obsession that speaks to you."

Give yourself permission to fly, trusting that even if you fall, you'll get back up. Give yourself permission to show up in life confidently. Give yourself permission to face your fear. Give yourself permission to know you, be you, love you, and do you. Give yourself permission...

Here is a story I love. It is a story of a woman's decision to answer the call and start walking in her purpose. I call it 'Permission Granted!'

I felt God was tapping me on the shoulder reminding me that this gift was waiting inside of me. Imagine if someone gives you a gift, specifically picked out and wrapped up beautifully for you. They're excited to give it to you and when they do, you put it on the table. A year later when they come to your house, the gift is still on the table, unopened. How offended would that person be?

I felt that way–that God has given me this amazing gift, along with the tools, couched in skills, abilities, and experiences.

Imagine me then wasting away in jobs I really don't want to be doing, knowing that there's so much more for me. When I come face to face with God, how could I possibly tell him I didn't have the courage to use the gift he placed in me? That doesn't bear thinking of. How dare I not use it to help elevate somebody who needs it in their life, and also, in the process, transform my own life?

But that takes courage because of all the head trash, all the limiting beliefs I was telling myself of who I was and who I couldn't be, based on what I thought I needed but didn't have in my arsenal.

Are you making room for your gift?

It wasn't until I got to a place where I challenged what I'd always believed about myself, where I was willing to disrupt my norm, that I could dismantle everything I'd ever thought about who I could or couldn't be and give myself permission. Permission to unwrap, unveil, and unleash my gifts. Permission to be used as a vessel to change other people's lives while transforming my own life. Permission to stop confusing being qualified with being equipped. I was already equipped to serve other people; I had experience: life experience, professional experience, personal experience. I had to bring all these things to the table to know that I was enough to serve someone else. You are sitting on what someone else is waiting for. They are waiting for that thing which you are discrediting and diminishing because you think it's not good enough. So you stay stuck and held hostage making it about you instead of releasing your ego, instead of realising that your message is bigger than your ego. You are already equipped to serve other people, and you can continue to learn and grow and serve people at a higher level.

"You were beautifully resourced to be the best you can be.
Use what you've got and be the best you can be."

As for me, for many years, I knew I was out of alignment, not using my gifts. I knew that I had more value than I was delivering. I knew there was more for me to do, but I didn't have the courage. I dimmed my lights. All the power was inside me, but I wasn't giving myself permission to unleash it to the world. It wasn't until I got to a place where the void in my heart and the voice in my head became so loud it was deafening. I was being pushed in the direction of my gift, but I kept running away.

It wasn't until I hit a mental brick wall that I gave myself permission to step out of the slow lane and step into my next level.

I came into my own when I became aware of my purpose and chose to live a life driven by that purpose. Have faith in your gift and give yourself permission to fly. Believe in yourself and bet on you.

Give yourself permission to show up in life confidently. Give yourself permission to face your fear. Give yourself permission to know you, love you, and do you. You were beautifully equipped and resourced to fulfill your purpose. Everything you need is within you. You are enough, just the way you are.

"Develop an attitude of optimism.
Believe it is possible."

You came here to do something. There are things you can do that you've never done before or maybe even considered before. We must live with a sense of urgency because every moment counts. We're in a place we've never been before. What's in you that you're able to do? This is the time to live your life in a way to deliver your breakthrough moments. Consider this in the various areas of your life. Look at ways to take your performance to the next level in every area of your life. Get out of your own way and step into your next level. Do it now! 'Sometime later' becomes never.

What changes do you want to make in your life? What things have you been talking about but haven't done because you've been operating at your current level? Now you're moving into the next chapter, you're taking things to another level. This next chapter, this next level will require a different strategy. Sometimes we need a different strategy to achieve our goal.

Life is for living, for loving, for being healthy, and for pursuing purpose. Being purposeful narrows your choices; it means you are intentional about your options. Live without a void in your life by following your passions, desires, and purpose. Everybody is born with a gift. Some people know right away, such as Nina Simone, the jazz and classical musician who started playing the piano before the age of 5. For some of us, it takes us a little while to recognise it, but recognise it we must! Rob the cemetery of your gifts, use them all up while you're alive.

"Don't die with your music still in you."
- Serena Dyer and Wayne Dyer

Do the same for the children around you. Expose them to as many activities, talents, and abilities as possible so that they can see themselves in other people. Some people don't know their talents right away because they have not been exposed or seen anyone doing what they love. Sometimes, even when they're exposed to it, they don't recognise the greatness they carry within them. Sometimes they don't get the opportunity to try, or sometimes they disqualify themselves from trying because they lack courage. Some people get sidetracked because they get busy with living their life instead of loving their life. They don't know what they can do because they have become busy surviving instead of living a life they love. This is the group to which I belonged and this is the group to which my message is directed.

Don't live a life that's not you and which doesn't represent the highest version of you. Live a life that will make the future you look with pride at the current you and say, 'You did well girl, you made me proud. I'm glad you chose me. I'm glad you gave us a chance.'

Before you make a decision, ask yourself, 'Is this going to bring out the best in me? Is this going to take my life in the direction that represents the highest version of me, or is this going to take me down a path that at some point in time I will regret that I made this choice?'

"Live a life that will make the future you say,
'Thank you for choosing me.'"

Life meets you where you are. Have a plan of action that expands your vision, upgrades your skillset, and extends and improves your sense of self. Spend some time sharpening your mind and growing yourself personally. Doing this fortifies the belief that you can do what you want to do.

The journey of working on yourself liberates you and gives you the keys to expand yourself, to get a larger vision of your life, and to stop living a small vision of yourself from where you are stuck, unable to move forward.

Some people are carrying within them greatness which is now dead, genius which is now dead, abilities and talents which need to be resurrected because they're dead. Don't let your talents and abilities die. Don't take them to the grave. Rob the cemetery of your gifts and live with a sense of urgency. Use your talents, your abilities, and your knowledge in a different way and become more impactful. We came here to create. We were created by the Creator to create. Live with a sense of urgency and create.

"If I had six hours to chop down a tree,
I'd spend four sharpening my axe."
- Abraham Lincoln, 1809 – 1865

10 Paths to Purpose

1. Listen to your inner voice; it is speaking to you from your heart. Our heart acts like an inner GPS. It's that wise voice that knows our desires, our passions, our dreams. When we have a desire, it's coming from a deeper level. To hear the message from the inner voice, we have to be still and listen. Your inner wisdom can't get through to you when you're busy. It speaks to you when you're quiet and listening. One way to achieve this is through meditation. Meditation and other techniques which help us connect with our inner self are included in *The Inner Sanctuary*. Use these techniques to get clarity and access to deeper wisdom.

2. Follow your passion. Joy and passion are signs of alignment with your purpose. Your passion is the fuel to your purpose. Simply put, 'passion is what gets you started, and purpose is what keeps you going'. https://www.theprofitablepassion. com/what-comes-first-passion-vs-purpose/

3. Purpose leaves clues. I believe that there's no such thing as a coincidence. You'll find that things seem to line up miraculously and you'll experience serendipitous meetings, phone calls, and so on, like you have a silent genie working diligently on your case.

4. Trust the process. Trust and believe that what you are seeking is meant for you and in time will find its way to you. This is a key principle I have learned in my life, as you will see in the next few pages.

"Your words should not negate, they should create."

5. Do not get frustrated or impatient at every bump in the road. Breathe. Handle this from a position of strength and trust that things will turn out well in the end. Know that in your heart you're already aligned with your purpose and it is making its way to you.

6. Clear the mental roadblocks. Ensure that your thoughts, words, and beliefs are not acting as blockers. Eliminate your fears and limiting beliefs and replace them with an empowering belief system. Close the door on your old beliefs and focus on seeing opportunities.

7. Don't worry about the 'how'. When you have a big desire that perhaps feels a little too big or even impossible, it's easy to get caught up on the how. It might even be what stops you from going after the things you want in the first place, because it doesn't feel realistic unless you have a strategically mapped-out plan. Don't worry about having all the answers in order to make progress. Just take the first step. You don't need to see the road ahead. Take the first step and the road will appear.

8. Surround yourself with the right people who support you in achieving your dream. Be a support to these people too.

9. Believe you have the ability to fulfill your purpose. Remember that you were created, equipped, and resourced for purpose. You possess everything you need to fulfill your purpose.

10. Relax. Your purpose, your desires, and your dreams are working just as hard to get to you. Don't focus on the promised pot of gold at the end of the journey. The journey is paved with diamonds.

"Think and speak what you seek until you see what you seek."

Spa
What is your Why?

Whatever you were created to become, you possess it now. Your purpose is timeless and unlimited. You cannot run out of it, but you can waste it by leaving it unused.

You are beautifully resourced and equipped with gifts to fulfill it.

What is your purpose? Do you want to write, sing, play music, foster children, teach, or perhaps, volunteer? It does not matter. What matters is that you discover and serve it to the world.

No one's purpose is any more or less meaningful than another's. Your job is to figure out what it is, honour it, and enjoy living a life in alignment with your values.

Gifts can never be learned, but they can be refined and developed.

Do not give your gifts to the graveyard. Nurture them, invest in them, and develop them.

Your gift is who you are and your gift makes room for you.

You are more powerful than you know.
Fear the day you find out.

- Amina

Here is a story about how our external circumstances can affect us:

Once upon a time, a daughter complained to her father that her life was miserable and that she didn't know how she was going to make it. She was tired of fighting and struggling all the time. It seemed that just as one problem was solved, another one soon followed.

Her father, a chef, took her to the kitchen. He filled three pots with water and placed each on a high fire. Once the three pots began to boil, he placed potatoes in one pot, eggs in the second pot, and ground coffee beans in the third pot. He then let them sit and boil, without saying a word to his daughter.

The daughter moaned and impatiently waited, wondering what he was doing. After twenty minutes he turned off the burners. He took the potatoes out of the pot and placed them in a bowl. He pulled the eggs out and placed them in a bowl. He then ladled the coffee out and placed it in a cup. Turning to her he asked. "Daughter, what do you see?"

"Potatoes, eggs, and coffee," she hastily replied. "Look closer," he said, "and touch the potatoes." She did and noted that they were soft. He then asked her to take an egg and break it. After pulling off the shell, she observed the hard-boiled egg.

Finally, he asked her to sip the coffee. Its rich aroma brought a smile to her face. "Father, what does this mean?" she asked. He then explained that the potatoes, the eggs, and the coffee beans had each faced the same adversity: the boiling water. However, each one reacted differently.

The potato went in strong, hard, and unrelenting, but in boiling water, it became soft and weak. The egg was fragile, with the thin outer shell protecting its liquid interior until it was put in the boiling water. Then the

78

inside of the egg became hard. However, the ground coffee beans were unique. After they were exposed to the boiling water, they changed the water and created something new.

"Which are you," he asked his daughter. "When adversity knocks on your door, how do you respond? Are you a potato, an egg, or a coffee bean? "

In life we all experience trials and tribulations. We experience circumstances which can break us. We may not always be able to control these circumstances; the only thing we can control is how we manage them. If we react to the event, it's in control and could potentially break us. This is living from the outside in. The external environment shapes us, moulds us, and breaks us. When we respond, however, we are in control, we hold the power. We control the situation by changing our perspective. We should strive to live like this. We become the master, we're the boss. A reaction may produce a positive or negative outcome, but a response produces an engineered outcome. Simply put, reacting is emotional and responding is emotional intelligence.

"A pessimist sees the calamity in every opportunity.
An optimist sees an opportunity in every calamity."
- Les Brown

For as he thinketh in his heart, so is he.

- Holy Bible, KJV, Proverbs 23:7

Be yourself:
everyone else is
already taken.

- *Oscar Wilde*

Our deepest fear is not that we are inadequate.

Our deepest fear is that we are powerful beyond measure.

It is our light, not our darkness that most frightens us.

We ask ourselves, 'Who am I to be brilliant, gorgeous, talented, fabulous?'

Actually, who are you not to be? You are a child of God.

Your playing small does not serve the world.

There is nothing enlightened about shrinking so that other people won't feel insecure around you.

We are all meant to shine, as children do.

We were born to make manifest the glory of God that is within us.

It's not just in some of us; it's in everyone.

And as we let our own light shine, we unconsciously give other people permission to do the same.

As we are liberated from our own fear, our presence automatically liberates others.

- Marianne Williamson

Trust The Process

My family and I lived in a small three-bedroom house in Stanmore, a suburb in the London Borough of Harrow in Northwest London. With two growing boys we had outgrown the quaint, cosy house and wanted to move to a bigger house with more space, in a great neighbourhood and closer to the children's school.

We identified our preferred location and contacted local real estate agents covering those areas to register our interest. It was 2003, before home search websites and the internet became commonplace, so we would be sent a list of all the properties that matched our criteria by post on a weekly basis.

Each week the postman would arrive with the listings and I'd look through them eagerly. Each week I was disappointed because the houses we were sent were either not big enough for our needs or were above our price point. After a few weeks I noticed that one particular agent kept sending through details of the same property. I called to let them know that we were not interested in the area in which the house was located and asked that they remove it from the listings we were sent. The lady I spoke to was pleasant and obliging, saying that she'd make a note on their records and I would no longer receive details of the property.

The following week I was surprised to see that the details of the same property had once again been sent for our review.

"I have a right to be wrong."
- Joss Stone

I called the agency and again explained that we were not interested in that location. Again, I was told that a note had been made on our records and we would no longer receive notice of the listing. In the meantime, eagerly, I kept awaiting details of properties in our desired location.

The following week, while I was in the driveway of my home, about to get in my car and leave to pick up my younger son from nursery, I spotted the postman coming up the road, dropping off mail. I waited to get our mail and when the postman put them in my hand I opened up the envelopes. By this time I was in the car, ready to drive away. There was one envelope from an estate agent, which I opened with great anticipation. In the envelope was just one sheet of paper with details of a listed property. Yes, you guessed it, it was the same property! The very same one I'd called about twice, asking for it not to be sent again. I looked at my watch, and noticing that I had a few minutes to spare, decided to drive by the property to take a look at it. The road it was on was on the way to the nursery anyway and I figured that if I saw it, I could convince the agency that it was a waste of their time and money posting it to us every week. In my mind, at best this was inefficiency by the agents, and at worst it was borderline harassment!

I'm sure you can imagine my shock when I drove onto the road the property was on. It was a beautiful tree-lined quiet cul-de-sac within a conservation area with enclosed meadows.

"Whenever you wake up is your morning."

84

It consisted of only a few houses of sizeable proportions surrounded by populated countryside. The road was serene and peaceful—great for raising children—and each house had its own unique architecture, many of which were originally part of a 1800s country estate. It was perfect! And it was beautiful.

It took a little while for me to regain my composure. To say I was flabbergasted would be a huge understatement. I called the agent immediately and set up an appointment to view the house. Fortunately, they didn't ask me about my previous calls asking them to stop sending me its details! I don't know if this was because of their level of inefficiency, if it had been part of their game plan, or if this was a divine instruction. I choose to believe it was a divine instruction.

I picked up my son from nursery and went back with him to view the house at the scheduled time. The inside did not disappoint. It was bright, airy and spacious, as lovely as the outside. After the viewing, I sat in the car, right outside the property, and called my husband at work saying, 'I've found our next home!' Three months later, after a smooth, hassle-free negotiation and legal process, we moved into the house and lived there happily for the next twelve years.

In life we have to learn to trust the process. This experience taught me that even though we plan and believe we know what we want, this is not always the case.

"Sometimes you have to get out of your own way."

We look at things from our own perspective and this can be narrow and limited. We do not always see the bigger picture. Trust the process and be prepared to change plans when you're called in a different direction. As I often say, prepare to change the plan even though the goal remains the same.

I often wonder about the chain of events that led to that house purchase. Despite all my efforts to sabotage the process, a mightier force than me was working behind the scenes, guiding, directing, and orchestrating like a silent choir master in a complex symphony.

Trust the process. Don't obsess about things you do not have any control over. Belief that all things work for good even though you might not be able to see how. Give up your right to be right and take the first step, allowing the journey to unfold as you go. In the words of Rumi, as you start to walk on the way, the way appears. Trust your journey, trust your heart, and trust your maker.

"Practice the pause.
When in doubt, pause.
When angry, pause.
When tired, pause.
When stressed, pause.
And when you pause, pray."
- Toby Mac

CHAPTER THREE

Love You

Life is an Adventure...Dare it

Life is a Beauty...Praise It

Life is a Challenge...Meet it

Life is a Duty...Perform it

Life is a Love...Enjoy it

Life is a Tragedy...Face it

Life is a Struggle...Fight it

Life is a Promise...Fulfill it

Life is a Game...Play it

Life is a Gift...Accept it

Life is a Journey...Complete it

Life is a Mystery...Unfold it

Life is a Goal...Achieve it

Life is an Opportunity...Take it

Life is a Puzzle...Solve it

Life is a Song...Overcome it

Life is a Spirit...Realise it

- Anon

Just The Way You Are

Many people disqualify themselves from the race of life before they have a chance to get started because they see themselves as less than who they are. They do not know the value they carry so they play small, they think small, and they act small. When you know who you are, you feel empowered. You recognise the strengths, the values, the gifts, and the talents that you carry. You recognise your worth. When you know your worth and you know the value you carry, it is easy to fall in love with yourself because you know you are precious. You are a diamond and your imperfections make you perfect.

I believe it is difficult to love yourself if you don't know who you are, because you cannot love something you don't know. You cannot love something if you don't know what value it carries.

Discovering who you are empowers you to fall in love with yourself, to embrace life and be your true, authentic self. For you to stand up in the world and own your space, own your truth, own your greatness and make yourself stand out, you must first love yourself. You cannot stand up for someone you do not love.

"The first person you need to fall in love with is yourself."

Before I took the time to learn about myself, I frequently moved from one great role to another, looking for the best boss, best team, best CEO, best organisation, or best sector, believing that what I was looking for would be found in the next role. I compared myself to other people who had worked in the same organisation for many years and I celebrated them when they clocked another year with the company. There was a lot of negative self-talk going on in my head. I didn't believe I was smart enough to push through the ceilings of the corporate world or to be the type of employee who gave their best years to an organisation. On one hand, I felt I was better than a paycheque, but on the other hand, I only saw my failures, weaknesses, limitations, and past mistakes. Worse, I was measuring my life and my successes using someone else's ruler.

It wasn't until I discovered myself that I could honestly say, 'This is me, warts and all'. Yes, I have flaws and weaknesses, but I also have great value. When I discovered that I am enough just the way I am, my self-worth, self-belief, and self-love grew. Every day, I say to myself, 'I am enough'. I urge you to try saying this to yourself in the mirror every morning.

To create the life of *your* dreams, you need to identify what you want. Be authentic and true. You are unique because there is only one you. The combination of your life, your story, your voice, your superpowers, and your talents, gifts, and abilities are unique to only you. They make up your DNA and should be used to contribute to the world—don't hide them away! You are unique and there's only one version of you. Anything else is a copy. Get to know and fall in love with the original.

"Spend time getting your body, mind, and spirit in alignment."

Spa
Just The Way You Are

It is important to know yourself; accept who you are and be happy in your skin, just the way you are.

Spend time alone, enjoying your own company.

Connect with yourself intimately by looking inwards to clarify your beliefs, values, dreams, and inspirations. Your dreams are often clues to your identity.

Love and enjoy your relationship with yourself so that anyone who enters your space is drawn to a world of happiness.

Fall in love with yourself, just the way you are.

Say to yourself every day, 'I am enough'.

Start a beautiful romance by loving yourself.

"Love never fails."

- Holy Bible, KJV, 1 Corinthians 13:8

You have value

Spend time discovering who you really are. Know and believe your worth or no one else will. Treat yourself with love and respect. Accept no less than you deserve, and others will treat you accordingly.

You are worthy

You, not anyone else, have the power and responsibility to make you happy. You decide your self-worth. Anyone else's love and desire for your happiness is a bonus.

You are lovable just the way you are. You do not have to be perfect. Perfection is an ideal, not a reality; therefore, pursuing perfection is a recipe for disappointment. When you love yourself, you will radiate joy, happiness, and confidence, which make you lovable. Focus on your positive qualities and fill your life with the things that bring you joy.

You are special

It is easy to treat yourself as an afterthought. Treat yourself like you're special. Fill your time with hobbies, passions, and activities that interest you. Indulge in self-praise, even in the small things. Continually develop your gifts, abilities, and talents to reach your maximum potential.

Speak peaceful and loving words about yourself to yourself. Speak like you matter, because you do.

"Love is a choice."

Let go of your past

Never be ashamed of your past, because it has brought you to where you are today. Learn from it and move on. Share the lessons learned from your experiences so others can avoid a similar fate. Remember that your story is not a burden but a weapon which serves as a blueprint, a survival guide for other people.

Change your perspective

View any weaknesses with compassion and try to change your perspective; flip it to see the positive. If, for example, you are always running late because you like to leave the house tidy before leaving home, appreciate that it means you return to a clean house after a long day. Instead of getting angry that you're running late again, decide to get up a little earlier to give yourself time to tidy up. Change your perspective to appreciate the benefits.

Help someone less fortunate than you

It is said that people who dedicate their lives to others are the happiest. Because happiness comes from the heart, sharing your blessings to make others happy, without any thought of a reward, also brings you joy. When you're feeling low, share your blessings with others to uplift and add value to both your life and theirs.

"Your story of what you overcame is not a burden but a weapon.
It will be a blueprint, a survival guide used to help other people."

Spa
Inspiration

1. Spend time alone, listening to yourself.
    Give yourself a chance to connect with yourself; learn
    what inspires you and get clarity on what is in your
    heart. While you're there, you'll find time for yourself.

2. Disconnect from your phone and social media.

3. Do the things that make you happy and bring you joy.

4. Take pleasure in the simple things and give thanks for
    everything.

5. Write ten characteristics about yourself that you love
    and appreciate. When you get to ten, keep going!

"Wait until you hear from your heart.
When you do, take action towards creating your next chapter."

Happiness is a choice

You have the power to create your own happiness. It is an attitude. You can decide to be happy and you should make it a habit to be happy. A happiness habit yields a happy life. Your thoughts and attitude determine your level of happiness. You can't be happy if your mind is filled with negative thoughts or negative beliefs. To get happiness from life you must put happiness into life. No one is in charge of your happiness except you.

Laughter is the best medicine

Relieves stress	Releases anger	Encourages forgiveness

Strengthens immune system (boosts mood, relieves physical tension)	Brings mind and body back into balance	Inspires hope

Lightens your burden	Strengthens relationships	Promotes wellbeing (supports physical and emotional health)

"Now and then it's good to pause in our pursuit of happiness and just be happy."
- Guillaume Apollinaire, 1880 – 1918

Give yourself permission to laugh at yourself. Laughter is no joke. Laugh all the time, the way children do; forget about the worries of the world and laugh. Lighten up, don't take things so seriously. Laugh yourself to your new life. Laughter is fun. And best of all, this priceless medicine is free!

The power of hobbies

Hobbies provide an outlet from our responsibilities and challenges. They allow you to relax, giving your inner mind the opportunity to emerge and speak to you. When you shift your concentration from your daily challenges, you hear your intuition and this experience can lead to a revelation!

Hobbies promote awareness, excitement, attention, satisfaction, and happiness; they reduce stress, depression, and negativity. So, don't be weighed down with nagging worries. Engage in interesting hobbies because they provide relaxation to a tired mind and lift your spirit, which brings you joy.

The actual hobby does not matter, as long as it gives you joy and is of interest to you. Hobbies distract the mind from day-to-day responsibilities and foster a fresh perspective to challenges.

"We don't stop playing because we grow old;
we grow old because we stop playing."
- George Bernard Shaw, 1856 - 1950

Spa
Happiness

Own your happiness and be responsible for doing those things that bring joy and peace into your heart, independent of people and circumstances.

Enjoy the journey. Don't wait until you get to the finish line, when you have the house, job, car, children, and the partner you desire; enjoy the process. Every day is special. Celebrate all your wins every day.

Balance work with play to give you a holistic and fuller life. Have fun, try new things, and embrace life.

Spread love outside of your immediate life through kindness and service. Be a blessing in the lives of others without expecting anything in return.

Spend more time outdoors. Fresh air produces a better mindset and can make you feel happy.

Listen to upbeat music.

Practice self-care.

Love yourself and enjoy your relationship with yourself so that people are drawn to your world of happiness.

Fill your mind with happy thoughts.

"Happiness is contagious."

Spa
Hobbies

Make room in your life for activities that nourish your soul and bring you joy.

Find something you enjoy doing and love yourself enough to spend time on it. Aside from the release and relief from your responsibilities, your mind gets the opportunity to relax, allowing the voice of your heart to speak louder and clearer.

Take time for you; do things you enjoy and focus on the vision of creating the life you desire.

Focus on and celebrate your wins, no matter how small.

Praise and congratulate yourself for your successes.

Spend time outdoors to see the beauty in your surroundings.

Forget about the past and the things you cannot change.

Practice meditation and mindfulness.

Protect your space, time, and energy by setting boundaries for people and activities.

Self-Care Is Self-Love

Self-care is not just about pampering

Self-care is about maintaining a healthy relationship with yourself, taking care of your home, your space, your health and wellbeing, and all the other areas of your life. Self-care produces positive feelings that boost your confidence and self-esteem. It reminds you of your importance and ensures your needs are met. Take time to do things that make you happy and bring you joy.

Take time to focus on you

Spend time alone, learn to enjoy your own company, and listen to yourself. Make every day count. Take care of yourself to maintain a good state of mind, one that empowers you to successfully navigate life.

Be protective of your time: make time for yourself, prioritise those things that are important to you, and engage in activities that fulfill you. Spend time developing your talents, skills, and abilities. Spend time nourishing your body and getting your mind and spirit in alignment.

"Do the things that bring you joy.
Take time out to give to yourself."

Spa
Self-care

Gets lots of sleep

Do something you enjoy

Light a candle

Journal

Make a delicious cup of tea

Wear something that makes you feel good

Develop yourself

Putting your home in order is self-care. They say one can tell the state of a person's mind by the state of their home. Calmness comes from clarity, and decluttering is essential for both your physical and mental wellbeing. Clutter can have an adverse effect on your health and can lead to anxiety and stress, so clear your physical space regularly.

Decluttering and discarding items when they are no longer needed decreases stress and anxiety levels and increases feelings of positivity and contentment. We experience a mind shift when we detach ourselves from things we don't need. Though it is not always easy, detaching ourselves lightens and energizes the mind.

"Your home reflects your mind."

Life is much easier when your home is clutter-free. All aspects of your life become sharper, more orderly, and more productive. And you'll be able to find things a lot quicker!

Spa
Clear the clutter

When you clear the excess clutter out of your life, you will notice the positive effects on your happiness, mental state, and overall wellness.

Declutter your home and your life to experience the positive changes that occur.

"Clear your space, clear your mind."

Everyday people

The people with whom we associate will have a great impact on our lives: our health, wealth, and wellbeing. You are no more than the relationships you surround yourself with, so make sure they are good ones. Our lives are usually a reflection of the expectations of our friends and peer group, as these are the people who have a large impact on the trajectory of our lives. To succeed in designing the next chapter of your life, it is essential that you surround yourself with a success team. This team is made up of people who believe in you, who challenge you to grow, and who help you to be the best version of you. They help you uphold your values and encourage you to achieve your goals and be the best you can be.

Get yourself a mentor, a coach, and an accountability partner and commit to these relationships. On the other side, be a member of someone else's 'everyday people' by being a person who helps them achieve their goals. Share your knowledge, skills, and assets. The more you help others overcome their obstacles, the easier it will be to overcome yours.

Make relationships count. Get nourishment from close relationships with your partner, children, family, and friends, because you cannot be fruitful by yourself.

"Love, hope and inspiration are like perfume. In spraying some on others, you can't help getting some on yourself."
- Les Brown

Spa
Everyday people

Are the people you align yourself with positive and uplifting? Do they achieve their own dreams?

Draw from people who also go after their own dreams.

We all have moments when we are not at our best, so ensure you have dependable friends with positive energy.

Sometimes you need to believe in someone else's belief in you until your own belief kicks in.

Know your tribe

We all need our tribe of 'everyday people'. People we can count on every day; they are our 'ride or die'.

Identify your everyday people, invest your time and energy, and nourish those relationships.

Just as important as identifying your tribe of everyday people is determining who will include you in their tribe of everyday people.

Whose standard are you raising?

Who can count on you? Who are you supporting?

Get in a tribe and get on a list.

Like attracts like

The more love, hope, and inspiration you give to others, the more you attract to yourself.

"Nourishing relationships are uplifting."

And now these three remain: faith, hope, and love. But the greatest of these is love.

- Holy Bible, KJV, 1 Corinthians 13:13

Don't waste time
complaining about
relationships that
are sucking the life
out of you when
you're the one
providing the straw.

- *Les Brown*

On 17 September 2018, my heart broke into a thousand tiny pieces all around me. It was the day my darling mum passed. My mum was 82 years old, and in the six or so years preceding her death, she'd suffered multiple strokes, a broken leg, and other ailments. I believe it was her heart that finally lost her the battle when on 11 August 2017 her soulmate, best friend, and husband of 59 years, my father, passed. On that day, the light in her eyes went out. On that day, she made her own plans to join him.

I think of my mum every day—her smile, her quiet but razor-sharp wit, her intuition, her guidance, her counsel, but most of all her friendship. As well as being my mother, she was also my mentor, coach, nurse, teacher, confidante, best friend, and unrelenting cheerleader. She never gave up on me, even on the occasions when I gave up on myself. She stood by me through thick and thin and loved me even when I didn't love myself.

It always amazed me how well she was able to stay positive and hopeful in all circumstances. We would talk for hours, often with me sharing with her whatever story of woe I was going through at the time, whether at school or work. Afterwards, she'd summarise the issue so succinctly then make a joke in her native Patois. She'd say, 'Don't worry Ene, dem is no dyam good. Dem is just like the Jarret dem!' This never failed to crack me. It was sure to make me feel better. Always. Every time.

"A mother is she who can take the place of all others
but whose place no one else can take."
- Cardinal Mermillod

Born and raised in Runaway Bay, St Ann's, Jamaica, she loved music and gardening. In the '70s, I was a young child growing up in GRA Ikeja, Lagos, Nigeria. On Sunday afternoons, my parents would unwind, relax, and enjoy the soulful sounds of Bob Marley, Peter Tosh, Harry Belafonte, Jim Reeves, and Lord Kitchener bellowing out from the sound system in our living room. Sometimes they would dance, my mum in her long Ankara dress and my dad in his dashiki shirt. Those were good times.

Humour is a non-negotiable ingredient of life in my family. My mum always had a funny anecdote and great one-liners. Reserved and quiet, she preferred to stay out of the limelight, especially in comparison to my dad, who was the life and soul of every party. My mum wasn't as naturally jovial and full of life as my dad, but she was every bit as funny, with a ready sense of humour reserved for her nearest and dearest. My dad would laugh heartily at the off-the-cuff remarks she often said under her breath. These quality one-liners were well-delivered, timely, and always hit home. Daddy would look at her quizzically when she delivered them, wondering at the deftness of someone so unassuming, with his eyes acknowledging that he recognised her as an equal in the high-stakes game of quick, cutting, humorous banter.

My mum was not always my best friend. As a child I thought she was overly strict. As I got older and became a woman myself, got married, and had children, my respect and admiration for her went through the roof. She turned into an angel in my eyes.

"A mother is your first friend, your best friend, your forever friend."
- Unknown

107

I often say that the best prescription for a child who complains about their parents is to have children of their own!

My mother was the best mother in the world. She was patient and full of unconditional love, and nothing—nothing—was too much for her. She was always there: a rock, a supporter, and an inspiration. She encouraged me to worry less, trust more, and develop faith. She always believed that things would get better, even in bleak and dark days. I don't know the source of her steadfast faith, but it was rock solid. She was my rock.

My mum had a quiet humility about her that made you want to be around her. She looked to her household and family; she was never influenced by the things of the world and never betrayed her love for her family. The adage 'cut your coat according to your cloth' could have been created by my mum. She didn't give any attention to what went on in other people's lives. Her only concern was how she maintained her own household.

It was my mum who helped me understand the importance of focussing on the positive instead of the negative of a person or situation. She would always say to me, 'Look for the blessing and use the good to paint over the bad'. This piece of advice is one I continue to live by.

"Of all the things my hands have held, the best, by far, is you."
- Unknown

A few months after my mum passed, I was clearing out old messages from my home phone voicemail and heard a message she'd left for me on my last birthday. I felt like I had won a million pounds. I made several copies of the message but I'm still unable to delete the original. That message will sit in my voicemail box for as long as I have a choice. I listen to it whenever I need comfort. Whenever I listen to it, I know that everything will be alright.

On the day she was reunited with her best friend, I imagine there was a steel band party in Heaven, where she and my dad were dancing and having a great time. I imagine my dad saying to her, 'Ah Jamo', as he fondly referred to her (a short form of Jamaican), 'what happened to you? I've been waiting for over a year'. My mum would smile and reply, 'Ah, I'm here now. I had to sort out the children. You know dem is just like the Jarret dem!'

My Mother

Who sat and watched my infant head
When sleeping on my cradle bed,
And tears of sweet affection shed?
My Mother.

When pain and sickness made me cry,
Who gazed upon my heavy eye,
And wept for fear that I should die?
My Mother.

Who taught my infant lips to pray
And love God's holy book and day,
And walk in wisdom's pleasant way?
My Mother.

And can I ever cease to be
Affectionate and kind to thee,
Who wast so very kind to me,
My Mother?

Ah, no! the thought I cannot bear,
And if God please my life to spare
I hope I shall reward thy care,
My Mother.

When thou art feeble, old and grey,
My healthy arm shall be thy stay,
And I will soothe thy pains away,
My Mother.

- Ann Taylor, 1782 – 1866

CHAPTER FOUR

Do You

"If a man does not keep pace
with his companions,
perhaps it is because he
hears a different drummer.
Let him step to the music he hears,
however distant or far away."

- Henry David Thoreau, 1817 -1862

Trust the Magic of New Beginnings

Sometimes a failure can leave us broken. A difficult situation that we think is so huge, it has the potential to break us. We cannot see a way out because we haven't got the skills or experience to deal with a challenge of this magnitude, and so we feel powerless. Have you ever been in a situation such as this? I have. This is a place I once lived. It's a street I call Despair.

It was 2001 and I was working as the Graduate & MBA Development Manager at arguably the world's most prestigious investment bank. My sons were incredibly young, six and three years old. We had a nanny who picked them up from school and nursery every day and looked after them in our home until I got home from work.

With the demands of a full-time job, I wasn't spending as much time with my children as I would have liked. I was missing out on them. To allow myself more flexibility, I decided to give up my job and start my own business. I love children's clothes, so I opened a childrenswear shop. Almost four years later, with high rent and rates and the trading uncertainty which has led to the gradual decline of the high street, my shop failed monumentally, leaving me over £100k in debt. It might as well have been ten million. It felt like that to me. I was deep in debt and well out of my depth.

The failure of that business dealt me a heavy blow. I thought I was ruined. I lost all hope and I couldn't see a future. There were days when I felt I couldn't carry on. I thought it was the end of me, and it very nearly was. I am ashamed to say that I was tempted to do something foolish. I considered taking my own life. Several times. My parents, my husband, and my two young sons are the reasons I didn't do it. One day my mum said to me, 'Who do you think is better able to look after the boys as well as you?' These words gave me the strength to carry on, to dig deeper. It was tough, though. I felt hopeless and helpless, and I lived in a permanent state of despair.

Some days were very bleak. My credit rating went from Excellent to Poor in what seemed like a minute. I went back to work but even with that, our expenses exceeded our income because of the debt. It was a huge burden on me. I carried the weight on my shoulders, the weight of the guilt and the weight of the shame for making my family go through this. They hadn't asked for this and they didn't deserve this.

Business failure can strip you of all self-respect. I was humiliated and ashamed. I was responsible for bringing this situation to my family, and that acknowledgement brought with it a deep sense of guilt, a special feeling of degradation, ineptitude, and despair. I had failed financially, personally, and professionally. I was a failure.

My husband and I took a long hard look at our finances and considered our options. No option was particularly pretty. We decided to get a second mortgage on our home in order to consolidate the debts and start afresh.

"Be wise enough to know when you need help.
Be brave enough to ask for it."

The only asset we had was our home, so by securing a second mortgage on it, we were effectively putting it in jeopardy. I don't know how many of you have ever had the awful experience of getting a second mortgage on your home. You feel worthless. And everywhere on the paperwork there are warnings about the risk of losing your home. Like you don't know!

With the encouragement of my sister, I started to draw strength from my faith. There were many days when this was almost impossible, but every so often, unrelated events occurred which I interpreted as definite signs from above. I needed these signs; I needed to know that I wasn't alone. I needed to know that God hadn't abandoned me. I needed hope.

The smiles on the faces of my sons were a source of strength and hope. I lived for those smiles. I clung on to life because of their smiles and hugs. They were too young to understand what was going on and I didn't want them to sense that there was a problem. This only added to my shame and feeling like I was a failure. I'd let them down. I believe that having your children feel disappointed in you as a result of your actions has got to be one of the most humiliating experiences a parent can have.

One day, as I was crying out for help from whoever cared to hear my wails, my tears left streaks as they rolled down my cheeks. I begged for a sign that everything would be fine. I begged for a sign that one day this would be behind us. I begged for a sign that the pain would go away and I'd be debt-free.

"Sometimes you have to borrow belief until your belief kicks in."

All I saw around me was debt and I needed hope. I was deep in sorrow, I was deep in prayer, I was deep in tears. Then I experienced something I can only describe as a vision. I 'saw' myself at the cash register in my shop. I was looking out of the big display window and stood, transfixed to the spot. On the other side of the road, walking towards my shop and looking intently at me, was a man I recognised as Jesus. He was wearing a white cloak tied at the waist and Roman sandals on his feet. He held my gaze as he approached my shop, as though letting me know that it was me he came for.

He walked towards my shop purposefully and steadily. When he was directly opposite the shop, he stopped, waiting for a break in the traffic before crossing the street. He crossed over, never dropping his gaze as he headed straight for the door of the shop. By this time I knew, without a doubt, that it was me he was coming for. I walked around from the cash register, towards the door. When he got to the door, he didn't come into the shop. He stood outside, waiting for me. I got to the door and opened it, and he put his hand out to me. I took his hand and stepped out of the shop.

When I awakened from my reverie I felt—no, I knew in my heart, that everything was going to be all right. From that point it was going to be all right. It was the sign I'd been waiting for. We would be fine. I was certain of that.

"Every storm runs out of rain."

- Maya Angelou

We slowly started chipping away at our debt, focussing on what needed to get done and setting about getting it done. And let me tell you, it wasn't easy, but we were determined. I took responsibility, knuckled down at work, and focused on paying off the secured loan.

Little by little, we chipped away at it, denying ourselves many pleasures of life such as vacations. Paying off the debt was our only purpose. We made overpayments to the consolidation loan whenever we could, by living on a tight budget and focussing on the goal.

By 2010, approximately 5 years after the business failed, we had paid off the consolidation loan. Everything was paid off: credit cards, store cards, and short-term loans. The only loan we had was the main mortgage on our home. We remain debt-free today. I have not had a loan, credit card, or any other financial obligation since then, aside from a residential mortgage. Now, the same banks which were constantly chasing us with repayment reminders are still chasing us, except now they're asking to extend us credit! 'No thank you Mr Bank, I'm doing well all by myself!' I say as I rip up the many letters we receive offering credit. It's interesting how banks want to lend money to people who don't need their money!

At that time I vowed never to run my own business ever again. Ten years later, I asked myself, 'Now what? Are you going to let one failure finish you off? You didn't fail, the business did. Get up, dust yourself off, and be the boss woman that you know you are. Live your life so it doesn't owe you any change.'

"This too, shall pass."

True strength is found not in being knocked down but in how you rise afterwards. Sometimes, people see you after you've risen again, after you've overcome. Things are going well for you and they think your life is perfect. They forget the periods of despair, of pain, of disaster, and of devastation. Your determination helps you look up, rise up, and start again, this time, stronger, wiser, and more powerful. This might look like a 'perfect life' to the unwitting onlooker, but they don't know what you've been through. Your pain is in your power, your strength, and your purpose. Your breakthrough, as they say, is in your breakdown.

"Your breakthrough is in your breakdown."

Don't Quit

When things go wrong as they sometimes will,

When the road you're trudging seems all up hill,

When the funds are low and the debts are high

And you want to smile, but you have to sigh,

When care is pressing you down a bit,

Rest if you must, but don't you quit.

Life is strange with its twists and turns,

As every one of us sometimes learns,

And many a failure comes about,

When he might have won had he stuck it out;

Don't give up though the pace seems slow,

You may succeed with another blow.

Success is failure turned inside out,

The silver tint of the clouds of doubt,

And you never can tell just how close you are,

It may be near when it seems so far;

So stick to the fight when you're hardest hit,

It's when things seem worst that you must not quit.

- John Greenleaf Whittier, 1807 - 1892

Whose Life Is It Anyway?

As I've said, it wasn't until 2020 that I asked myself, 'What is the point of having this experience, with all that I have learned the hard way, the tears I have shed and the lessons I've learned, if not to use it to help people?' I have learnt that my story is not a burden, but a weapon to be used as a blueprint, a survival guide to help other people going through similar circumstances.

As I write this chapter it is January 2021 and we have regained everything we lost, many times over. They say that a setback is a set-up for a comeback. Oh yes it is! And there is no testimony without a test.

On the days when you're down and you feel low, you may need to borrow someone else's belief in you until your own belief kicks in. You may be down but you are not broken. Never try to solve a temporary situation with a permanent solution.

I want to encourage you, if you're going through adversity or challenges, to think of your life as a book with different chapters. Today is the end of the current chapter and tomorrow, tomorrow you start the next chapter. We can't start a new chapter if we keep re-reading the last one. We've read it enough times, it's time to move on. The difference is that in this chapter, this new chapter, you are in control. You are the author of your story. You are the hero of your life. You need to write the story the way YOU want it to go.

"When you're going through adversity, keep going."

So, hold your head up high, take a beautiful-looking pen and start writing your next chapter. It's your story and you're sticking to it!

In the words of Rumi, whatever you are seeking is also seeking you. Three months after I decided to leave my corporate job and become a speaker and coach, and two months after I started being mentored by the legendary Les Brown, I got the incredible opportunity to share my story on his global, virtual stage. In the words of the legend himself, 'It's Possible!'

I see my story not as a burden, but as a weapon. I want it to serve as encouragement to others. If I could get through those very bleak days of defeat, of hopelessness, of despair, of devastation, then so can you. As they say, when you're going through adversity, keep going!

I learned so many lessons about life, about love, and about myself from this experience. If I were asked to share my top three lessons, I'd have to request to share four. These four principles have become my life tenets. I figure that if they could get me through the darkest days of my life, they can take me over the line to my next destination.

A – **ACCEPT RESPONSIBILITY** by acknowledging that while you are not always in control of the things that happen to you, you are 100% in control of how to respond to these things. Give up excuses and complaining, take control of your response, and remember that 'this too, shall pass'.

"Live from the inside out and not outside in."

It is your life and you have to direct it and not let external factors move you out of alignment with who you are and where you want to go. Take responsibility for where you are and for your next move.

B – **BELIEVE** in yourself and in your own power. Work on developing an unwavering faith. Belief is a powerful force of trust, hope, and faith in the unseen, even if the reality is different. In the words of Henry Ford, 'Whether you think you can or you think you can't, you're right.' Think you can. Say to yourself, 'Maybe. Just maybe, it's possible.' When you're feeling out of your depth, believe in someone else's belief in you until your own belief kicks in.

C - Find the **COURAGE** to never give up and to rewrite the story of your life. You are the author of your next chapter and the hero of your story. Develop the courage to always be YOU. You are unique and there is only one version of you. Do not allow yourself to be an extra in the movie of your life. Find the courage to develop a grateful heart.

D – **Determination** decides destination. Decide to be the captain of your ship of life and commit to it. Be clear on what exactly it is that you want and what you do not want. Be determined to take action on what you create in your life and how you respond to external events and circumstances. In life we face circumstances and events over which we have no control. Choose how to respond to these circumstances. The power lies not in the level of control you have but in your response.

"Respond, don't react."

Finally, be grateful in and for all things. Gratitude helps to focus the mind and we should remember the blessings in our lives. In my case it was my family. My husband, my sons, my parents, and my siblings. They were the reason I hung on. They helped me stay focussed on the future. They carried me when I couldn't stand. On my darkest days, during my worst nightmares, my husband's calm and firm support was a rock to lean my weak heart on. If I ever needed a moment to demonstrate steadfast love, that was it. I knew then that he was a keeper. That was one of the first blessings I recognised and held on to, to get me out of the pit I was living in.

Develop an attitude of gratitude and give thanks for everything that happens to you, no matter how challenging that is. Have faith, knowing that every step forward is a step toward achieving something bigger and better than your current situation. In life we are presented with God-ordained opportunities brilliantly disguised as challenges. Look for the opportunities in your challenges.

Don't let circumstances get in the way of your action. When you're not stepping out, moving towards your dream, your dream is watching you. It is calling out to you, trying to reach you, trying to get your attention, saying, 'I'm here, I'm here, I've been trying to reach you, I've been calling out but you keep ignoring me'.

"Life will always be to a large extent what we ourselves make it.."
- Samuel Smiles

Your head, the voice of reason, the logical voice in you, gives you all the reasons why you should stay where you are. It tells you that you're fine right where you are. It has a hold on you because it knows your past and uses whatever ammunition it can to hold you captive. It is protecting you from getting hurt from defeat, from failure. It tells you to ignore your dream, saying to it, 'Be quiet! I'm fine here, don't rock the boat. Leave me alone.'

After a while you don't even hear the voice of your dreams anymore. You ignore your dreams because if you don't, you'll have to act on them. For a while it becomes easier to quieten them than to acknowledge them, but they find other ways to get your attention. These ways include making you feel stuck, dissatisfied, unfulfilled, frustrated, and empty.

You have to give up the common, mediocre part of you and trust yourself. A lot of people don't trust themselves. They don't know that they were born with the stuff they need to do what they're supposed to do. It is your right to have your dream. You don't get the dream, the desire, the passion to do something if you don't also have what it takes to do it. Remember, when you were created, you were equipped and resourced to be everything that you were born to be. Your dreams and passions are not an accident, they are your higher life calling you.

"Some people have thousands of reasons why they cannot do what they want to, when all they need is one reason why they can."
- Willis R. Whitney

It is your right to have your dream, and you have everything to need to fulfill your dream. If you didn't, you wouldn't have the dream. Your heart knows your dream and the possibilities, but your head tells you to be logical. It discourages you from doing what you want. Remember, your head knows your past and your present, and your heart sees the possibilities of your future.

Some people come up with all the reasons why they can't do what they want to do but don't try to think of a single reason why they can. They talk about everything going on in their life—their children are too young, they're too old or too young, they're married, they're single, they haven't got the financial means. They start foretelling their future, start saying what is not going well for them. They rarely talk about what they have or anything positive in their lives. If you look for reasons to put off going for your dream you will find them. Life will give you reasons.

People who accomplish their dreams don't have any more reasons for stepping towards their goals, they have the willingness and faith to give all their mental energy to the positive. They are willing to give their gift a chance.

Be your own cheerleader and come up with a reason why you can do it. A reason why your dream is a possibility. Your dream is calling you, it's waiting for an answer now. You have to determine how to answer, to dig deeper and to find strategies on how to make it happen.

"Nothing happens by itself, all will come your way once you understand that you have to make it come your way by your own exertion."

- Ben Stein

Get whatever help you need to overcome the struggles and obstacles you encounter. It's your life and it is your responsibility to live a life that represents you—not what people tell you, not what the environment tells you, not what your circumstances tell you.

Despite what happens, know that everything will be all right. Say to yourself, 'I'm going to be all right'. Be assured, feel it in your spirit. As you begin to look at where you want to go, know that you have a certain spirit about you, it's a certainty in your mind, in the air that you breathe.

Develop a faith, a belief, a hope that you and your dreams matter. Believe that you are special. This comes from quiet contemplation, knowing that you have something to do in life. Recognise that life is a gift and each day is a special gift. Each day is a new opportunity to go after your dream.

Look at your dreams, look at where you want to go, and know that it's on you to develop a path to get you there. Along the way you'll need to navigate the storms of life, your defeats, your failures, your mistakes, and your past. Your life is in your hands. You've got the power to have the life you want, the power to choose if this is the person you want to be. You've got the power to take yourself to another level. If you know there's more for you, you've got the power to be more. It's in you already, you need to bring it out. You are stepping to the beat of a different drummer. Let life use you up. Give yourself up to be used.

"You've got the power!"

You have the power to create the life you want to live. Dig deep, find that power, and develop it. Find the mental resolve. You have it and it will not let you down. Trust yourself, for you are more powerful than you know. You have to believe that things are going to get better, in spite of what you're going through. Refocus your mind. Look back on your life and see how far you've come, what you've overcome, the things you have been through. Take your strength and courage from these memories; let them give you hope. Stand firm in the belief that if you could get through these things, you can get through whatever you're dealing with now.

Whatever your current situation, know that it will pass. You have greatness within you. Do not allow yourself to be defined by your failures, mistakes, or circumstances. So, let go of the past. Tomorrow, start writing the next chapter.

"You cannot go back and make a new start, but you can start from now and create a new ending."

- Unknown

Vulnerability

Vulnerability is our strength, courage, and inspiration.

It's sharing our stories of heartache, pain, and rejection.

Our struggles, our burdens, our imperfections

and how we overcame despite our own objections.

I've learnt that my story is not a burden but a weapon

to use to help others going through depression.

Smile dear friend, know that this too shall pass

And when it does, you'll be moved up to the next class

where you'll sit, ponder, and reflect

how you came through bruised, confused, but not wrecked.

Then it's your turn to coach, teach, and mentor

those coming behind, in their own state of uproar.

Life is sweet, how can it not be?

When I look in your face and I see me.

Matching scars and bruises tell of our strength

And if I could, I'd do it all again.

The chance to turn around and throw a lifeline in to help

is far greater than any, any pain that I felt.

- Ene Obi

Spa
Do You

Authenticity means that we face life with boldness, openness, and honesty. It requires courage and confidence to be authentic, to stand out and do things others may not understand or may even criticise. We shouldn't pretend to be someone we're not.

We should be confident and secure in who we are, even if we're different from others.

Develop the courage to show up powerfully. When we are authentic, we inspire and empower others to do the same.

Embrace your uniqueness and shout from the rooftops, 'This is me!'

The best relationship you can have is the one with yourself. Enjoy being with yourself and being in your own space.

You should not apologise for being you.

What do you enjoy doing? How do you want to spend your time? What passions do you have? Find them and do them!

The best way you can serve the world is by being the best version of you.

So, start with yourself. Develop yourself, your gifts, and your talents and serve them to the world.

Start with your smallest sphere of influence—you and your family. Make an impact on the lives of those closest to you and then serve the world.

Put yourself at the top of your 'to-do' list.

Identify Your Magnificent Obsession

What are your dreams? The big dreams. Have a vision of a dream that you want for your life. Be fully committed to that dream. Live out of your imagination and not your past.

Everything you need to succeed is inside of you, just listen to your heart and trust it. Here's the thing: you don't have to know where this next chapter is going, you just need to start writing it.

Paint a picture of your perfect day
You don't have to have all the answers, for as you move forward, things will begin to move in your direction, and doors will open for you. Start over by writing your thoughts and goals to create a new script for your life as you'd like to see it.

Sometimes, when we reach for our goals and dreams we may not succeed by using a particular approach. When this happens, some people stop altogether. They become discouraged, so they give up. They're doing things in a certain way, believing it is the only way, so they use the same approach over and over again. Sometimes it may be necessary to try different things. If you fail using one approach, try a different way—but don't stop trying. Don't give up. Develop the mental resolve and willingness to learn, adapt, and adopt. This is 'breakthrough thinking'; it is the way to think to achieve a breakthrough.

"All our dreams can come true, if we have the courage to pursue them."

Sometimes things don't happen the way we'd like them to and we experience challenges, setbacks or even failure. Sometimes in life we are presented with God-ordained opportunities brilliantly disguised as challenges. When you experience a challenge, reframe the event and look for the opportunity. A setback is an opportunity to regroup and return. Some people say a setback is a set-up for a comeback! A failure is experience, and events are whatever we tell ourselves they are. Flip the narrative and change the script you have in your head then watch how your new perspective will deliver a different outcome.

The plan may change but the goal remains the same
A few days ago I caught a small piece of a Champions League football match my husband and sons were watching on television. (For clarity, by 'football' I mean 'soccer'.) Living in a house with men who are football-mad, a lot of my analogies and references come from football.

There was much excitement from my husband and sons as one of their favourite strikers had the ball and was heading to place it neatly at the back of the opponent's net. Defenders were coming quick and fast to take the ball off the striker. He was soon outnumbered with at least six defenders rounding up on him. He looked to his left, then to his right, looking for his teammates, looking for support and reliable feet to pass the ball to. Because he was so fast, his teammates were behind him, picking up their pace to get to him as quickly as possible.

"A step backward after making a wrong turn is a step in the right direction."
- Kurt Vonnegut Jr.

They saw that he was in a good position but needed back-up. He kept moving forward without losing possession of the ball, all the time looking around for support. As he used all the energy he had to maintain pace and possession of the ball, his face scrunched up to show the power, focus, and determination to score a goal. Just as he got into the box, a defender came in for a rough tackle but was a fraction of a second late. The quick thinking and deft judgement of the striker allowed him to see what was about to happen and he swiftly passed the ball to one of his teammates who had caught up with him. He offloaded the ball and with one touch by his teammate, it was placed neatly into the back of the net. I am certain that the raucous celebrations, hand-clapping and back-slapping by my men could have been heard for at least 30 miles.

To maximise his impact, the striker evaluated different approaches before deciding on the one he thought was likely to produce the desired result. In order to give his team a chance to score a goal, he came up with a new plan when he experienced a difficult situation. He didn't give up saying, 'Oh what's the point? Since I can't score I might as well call it a day and go home'.

Sometimes we need to take a fork in the road or even go backwards in order to regroup and come back stronger. Just because you didn't succeed the first time doesn't mean it can't be done by you. Just because the approach you're using now hasn't worked doesn't mean it won't work in the future or that no other approaches will work.

"For where your treasure is, there your heart will be also."
- Holy Bible, KJV, Matthew 6:21

130

Try a different approach. Get some help if you need it. Asking for help does not make you weak, it helps you remain strong. And don't stop until you get it. Remember, it's not about what happens to you; what matters most is what happens in you. Change your inner game.

In the heart of each of us is the voice of who we really are. Sit quietly and listen to that still inner voice of your heart, because it wants to be heard. Trust the voice and listen to the instructions it gives you. That is the voice of the genuine you. This voice will perhaps be the only guide you will have, and if you do not hear it, you will continue to be pulled by someone else's strings. Sit quietly until you hear it, for it will surely speak.

Don't apologise for your dreams

One Sunday, my nieces came over to the house for lunch. While we were eating, my son and nieces asked about how I was getting on with my new career. They wanted to know about my future plans. Timidly, I said, 'Well, you know, what would be nice is, well, I was thinking perhaps maybe, I'm not 100% sure but maybe I could perhaps, well, write a book.' My husband looked at me and said, 'Why are you apologising for your dream? Why? If you want to write a book, write a book!' Boom!

In that moment I realised that I was seeking encouragement and other people's acceptance of my dream. I hadn't yet given myself permission to go after my own dream! That day I decided to give myself permission for all my dreams and to take responsibility for making them a reality.

"You are enough, you know enough and you have all that you need."

Your dreams are valid. The only person who needs to grant you permission to go for them is the person you see when you look in the mirror. We should not apologise for our dreams. We should not treat ourselves as an afterthought. Give yourself permission to soar. You have so much potential. Become all of who you were divinely created to be.

Give yourself permission to create the next great version of yourself. You have the power to rewrite your story and untangle yourself from what restrains you. Give yourself permission to fly. This is your time. Believe in you! It's not over! Bet on you! Start today.

"I don't like to gamble
but if there is one thing
I am willing to bet on, it's myself."
- Beyoncé

"Never let anyone steal your dreams, including you."

Never give up on your dreams. Here is a beautiful story I'd like to share:

There is a story of a young man named Monty Roberts, who was the son of an itinerant horse trainer. As a result, Monty's education was continually interrupted. When Monty was a senior, he was asked to write a paper about what he wanted to be when he grew up.

That night he wrote a seven-page paper describing his goal of someday owning a horse ranch. He wrote about his dream in great detail and even drew a map of a 200-acre ranch, showing the location of all the buildings, the stables, and the track. He also drew a detailed floor plan for a 4000 square foot home that would be located on the ranch.

He put a great deal of his heart into the project and turned in the paper the next day. Two days later he received his paper back. On the front page was a large red F with a note from his teacher that asked Monty to see him after class. Monty went to the teacher after class as instructed and asked why he had received the failing grade.

The teacher said, 'This is an unrealistic dream for someone like you. You have no money. You come from an itinerant, poor family with few resources. Owning a horse ranch such as this requires a lot of money. There is no way you could ever achieve this dream.' Then the teacher told him he would reconsider the grade if the paper was rewritten with a more realistic goal.

Monty went home and thought long and hard about what to do next. He asked his father what he should do. His father said,

'Son, you will have to make up your own mind on this. It is a very important decision for you.' Finally, after careful thought, Monty turned in the same paper, making NO change. His remark to the teacher was, 'You can keep the F and I'll keep my dream.'

As the story goes, the boy, Monty Roberts, now owns a horse ranch in California and allows his home to be used for fundraising events for at-risk youth. His home is 4000 square feet and sits in the middle of his 200-acre ranch. He still has that school paper framed over the fireplace.

The best part of the story is that two summers ago that same schoolteacher brought thirty kids to camp out on this ranch for a week. When the teacher was leaving, he said, 'Look, Monty, I can tell you this now. When I was your teacher, I was something of a dream stealer. During those years I stole a lot of kids' dreams. Fortunately, you had enough gumption not to give on yours.' (https://digitalsparkmarketing.com/never-give-up-on-your-dreams/)

'There is freedom waiting for you,
On the breezes of the sky,
And you ask, "What if I fall?"
Oh but my darling,
What if you fly?'
- Erin Hanson

"You can't start the next chapter of your life if you keep re-reading the last one."
- Michael McMillian

134

All men dream but not all equally.
Those who dream at night,
in the dusty recesses of their minds,
wake up to find it was all vanity.
But the dreamers of the day are dangerous,
for they may act their dreams with open eyes,
and make things happen.
- T.E Lawrence, 1888 - 1935

Spa

Now is the time to pick up your magic pen and begin to write in your beautiful journal. What do you want to write? What do you see for yourself? Don't try to figure out a job, a business, a responsibility, or a role. What belongs on this page are those dreams that you have for yourself and your life. And all that's required to start writing is to start saying yes instead of telling yourself no.

This is the moment to write your next chapter. You're not too late, you're right on time.

Paint a picture of a perfect day for you.

Follow your heart, it knows the way.

Write a letter to your future self. Imagine that when your future self reads it, it will say to your present self, 'Thank you for betting on us'.

All you need is a blank page and a pen.

"Today is the first day of the rest of your life, start writing it."

I bargained with Life for a penny,
and Life would pay no more,
however I begged at evening,
when I counted my scanty store.

For Life is just an employer,
he gives you what you ask,
but once you have set the wages,
why, you must bear the task.

I worked for a menial's hire,
only to learn, dismayed,
that any wage I had asked of Life,
Life would have willingly paid.

- Jessie Belle Rittenhouse
1869 - 1948

Picture this...

It is 2025 and you are being interviewed.

You're asked to describe your life over the past 5 years.

What will you say?

"And suddenly you know it's time to start something new and trust the magic of beginnings."
- Meister Eckhart, 1260 - 1328

You cannot go back and make a new start, but you can start from now and create a new ending.

Today

Today is ours, let's live it
And love is strong, let's give it
A song can help, let's sing it
And peace is dear, let's bring it
The past is gone, don't rue it
Our work is here, let's do it
Our world is wrong, let's right it
The battle hard, let's fight it
The road is rough, let's clear it
The future vast, don't fear it
Is faith asleep? Let's wake it
Today is ours, let's take it

- Beah Richards, 1920 – 2000

CHAPTER FIVE

Affirmations For Living Your Best Life

―

The Power of 'I Am'

T he words, 'I am' are immensely powerful because what we say after these words defines who we are.

Words are like electricity; they have creative power to materialise what we say into our lives, so they can be dangerous if used in the wrong way. Whatever we think and say, we become. So, if you say, 'I am so clumsy', or 'lazy, poor, fat, unlucky', you are inviting those attributes into your life.

We use the power of 'I am' abusively when we say harsh, negative words to ourselves about ourselves. Although we wouldn't speak such negativity to another person, we feel no compunction speaking such self-destructive thoughts. Once they become our reality, we reinforce these attributes until they become a perpetuating, self-fulfilling prophecy.

Be careful about what follows your statements of 'I am'. Send out new invitations with empowering words describing how you want to see yourself and to be seen by others.

Strong, positive affirmations are a powerful means of self-transformation and can help you create the life you desire. You can purposely take the limiting ideas, negative beliefs, and self-talk you have adopted over the years and accepted as true and replace them with positive statements that assert who you want to be. The repetition of the ideas of the affirmations act directly on our emotions and our feelings. They go into the subconscious mind and get fixed there. Then, they penetrate to the very depths of our subconscious minds and control our behaviour, which produces the results we get in our lives.

Use these affirmations to help you describe your aspirations and desires. Choose the ones that resonate with you and meditate on them. You can also create your own affirmations, using the following guidelines:

Principles for Affirmations
Use these 3 Ps to create your own affirmations:

1. Personal: start with 'I am'. The mind sees any sentence that starts with 'I am' as an instruction and gets to work to make it a reality.
2. Present tense: write as though it has already happened, for example, 'I am at my ideal weight of *ideal weight*'

3. Positive: make them positive or affirmative, stating what you want, not what you do not want.

   For example, 'I am fit and healthy', instead of 'I am not ill'

Review your affirmations regularly and say them out loud at least twice a day, first thing in the morning and again before you go to bed. As you read, feel the emotion of already being in possession of the quality or characteristic of the affirmation.

If you repeat your affirmations every morning and night for a month, they will become an automatic part of your thinking and will now be embedded into your psyche. You are magnificent and you are a masterpiece. Tell yourself that until you believe it.

1. I am enough.
2. I am worthy of love.
3. I am worthy of the positive changes in my life.
4. I am authentic and willing to let go of who I think I should be to become who I really am.
5. I am unique and always show up powerfully as myself. The original is the best and anything else is a copy.
6. I am equipped and resourced for everything I need to fulfill my purpose.
7. I am worthy of forgiveness and healing.
8. I am in control of my words, thoughts, and actions.
9. I am blessed with many talents, gifts, and abilities.
10. I am in possession of everything I need to fulfill my purpose.

11. I am pursuing my purpose and destiny.

12. I am patient, I am kind, I am merciful, I am true, I am certain, and I am wanted.

13. I am centred, peaceful, and grounded.

14. I am happy in my happiness.

15. I am aligned with my purpose.

16. I am resilient and calm in a storm.

17. I am dependable and successful.

18. I am disciplined, reliable, and valuable.

19. I am open to receiving unexpected opportunities.

20. I am talented, confident, and wise.

21. I am strong, I am powerful, and I am grateful.

22. I am enough, I am worthy, and I have value.

23. I am constantly renewed to be the best I can be for where I am in my life.

24. I am vibrant, happy, and full of life.

25. I am a masterpiece and one of a kind. The original is the best and everything else is a copy.

26. I am willing to evolve and develop to suit the next version of who I am.

27. I am ready to share my gifts with the world.

28. I am strong, anointed, and inspired every day.

29. I am being all that I was made to be in every area of my life.

30. I am passionate and fulfilled about what I do.

31. I am able to create a life I love.

32. I am so happy and grateful that the source of my prosperity is within me.

33. I am compassionate with myself and with others.

34. I am influential and respected in my field.

35. I am worthy of love and belonging.

36. I am willing to let go of who I was and become who I need to be for the next version of me.

37. I am in perfect harmony with my mind, soul, and body.

38. I love and treasure my body.

39. I am healthy and feed my body with love and nutrition.

40. I am healthy, fit, and active

41. I am at peace with myself.

42. I am beautiful and allow my true self to flourish.

43. I am growing stronger physically, emotionally, and mentally, every day.

44. I am able and willing to tell myself I love myself.

45. I am blessed and highly favoured.

46. I am grateful for each moment.

47. I am happy and excited being who I am.

48. I am love, I am lovable, and I deserve love.

49. I am whole and I am enough.

50. I am beautiful just the way I am.

51. I am strong, powerful, and able.

52. I am enough, I know enough, I'm good enough, I have enough to start right now.

53. I am free, I am powerful, I am love, I have value, I have purpose.

54. I am empowered to create and live a fulfilled and abundant life.

55. I am prosperous.

56. I am grateful for my journey and its lessons.

57. I am fulfilling my destiny.

58. I am willing to ask for help when I need it, not because I am weak, but because I want to remain strong.

59. I am equipped to fulfill my purpose.

60. I am valuable; I have meaning and purpose.

61. I am so happy and grateful that all that is possible for anyone is possible for me.

62. I am worthy, and good things are happening to me.

63. I am valuable, I am abundant, and I am powerful.

64. I am the designer of my destiny and the author of my story.

65. I am full of energy and excitement for the life I am creating.

66. I am exactly where I need to be and I trust the process of my journey.

67. I am bold, I am courageous, and I am optimistic.

68. I am living to my full potential and excited about my future.

69. I am grateful for my healthy body which does everything I need it to do.

70. I am grateful for my blessings every day. I have everything I need to create the life I desire.

71. I am expecting the best, believing it is making its way to me.

72. I am joyfully living the life I love and deserve.

73. I am living a life that represents the highest form of who I am.

74. I am seeing the possibilities of all that I can be.

75. I am so happy and grateful that my body is fit and healthy.

76. I am so happy and grateful that everything I am seeking is seeking me.

77. I am so happy and grateful that I am exactly where I need to be in my life.

78. I am so happy and grateful that I am worthy to follow my dreams and manifest my desires.

79. I am so happy and grateful that I am surrounded by love and I give love in return.

80. I am so happy and grateful for the abundance of love flowing into my life.

81. I am so happy and grateful for all of life's blessings coming to me.

82. I am so happy and grateful that I step out of my comfort zone with courage, consistency, and confidence.

83. I am so happy and grateful that my happiness depends on me and no one else.

84. I am so happy and grateful that I have the power to create change.

85. I am at the right place, at the right time, doing the right thing.

86. I am so happy and grateful that when I take the first step the road opens up before me.

87. I am so happy and grateful that I give myself permission to be the best that I can be.

88. I am so happy and grateful that I choose faith over fear.

89. I am happy and grateful that I have everything I need to be successful.

90. I am so happy and grateful that I surround myself with positive people who support me and lift my energy.

91. I am so happy and grateful that I bring self-love and compassion into my life.

92. I am so happy and grateful that I see every challenge as an opportunity for God.

93. I am so happy and grateful that all is well in my world; I feel safe and secure.

94. I am so happy and grateful that I let go of all that does not serve me or align with who I am.

95. I am so happy and grateful that my life is full of purpose and passion.

96. I am excited to take continuous action towards completing my actions to achieve my goals.

97. I am so happy and grateful that I communicate with honesty, kindness, and compassion.

98. I am so happy and grateful for my healthy body, which heals on its own.

99. I am so happy and grateful that I am more powerful and have more potential than any circumstance, situation or condition.

100. I am blessed and highly favoured.

CHAPTER SIX

The Inner Sanctuary

12 powerful processes to connect with yourself
and create the life you desire.

---

12 Powerful processes

The power of...

Daily Habits	Mindfulness
Gratitude	Scripting
Goals	Asking For Help
Service	Forgiveness
Silence	Accept Responsibility
Meditation	Vision Boards

No single technique is a magic pill for success, but regular practice of these processes has many benefits, including self-discovery, clarity, gaining new perspectives, stress relief, and manifestation.

Daily Habits

Our habits create our future, so we need to pay close attention to our daily actions and develop habits that nurture our mind, body, and spirit.

Develop a morning ritual—the Hour of Power (HOP)—to include gratitude, which fortifies your spirit, meditation, mindfulness, scripting, and affirmations. This sets the tone for the rest of your day and will help you focus on improving your life. Read affirming and uplifting words for at least 30 minutes daily and use any down time as an opportunity to strengthen your mind and body.

Spend time being still. This gives you the opportunity to get your body aligned with your mind and spirit. Ensure that you complete your morning routine of fortifying your mind with empowering, inspirational, and positive messages before reading the newspaper, watching television, or checking electronic devices. Minimise the amount of time you spend watching or listening to negative, depressing news.

Television has so much negativity and round-the-clock news of doom and gloom. Negativity is disempowering and limiting, so for the sake of your wellbeing, restrict the time spent watching television. Instead, engage in activities that are positive, productive, and empowering. Whatever entertains you shapes you, so it's wise to monitor how you spend your time.

Reading stimulates the imagination. Read uplifting, inspirational words every day to train your brain to consider wider possibilities in your life. Inspirational music is also powerful.

"Fill your mind with positive words and music."

Gratitude

Gratitude erases all negativity and depression because gratitude cannot reside in the same space as either of these. Gratitude helps us to remember our good fortune. It shifts our focus from our challenges and reminds us of the greatness of our lives while keeping the door open for more blessings.

Gratitude changes your perception, and your perception changes your existence. Whatever you feed your focus expands, so the more things you think of to be grateful for, the more things you'll see to be grateful for.

It is easy to get consumed with the pressures and challenges of life, but the practice of gratitude is not an option; it is a necessity. There are opportunities to practice gratitude every day in every area of life.

So, no matter what situation you're facing, no matter how grave or hopeless, it is important to remember what you do have. Write it down. Writing helps you to focus and forces you to concentrate.

Every day, reflect on what you are grateful for in your life by thinking of the people, circumstances, events, and experiences in your life. The more things you think of, the more you'll remember. Write them all in your gratitude journal.

"Gratitude is an attitude."

Gratitude exercise

1. The everyday things. These are the simple life pleasures which we often take for granted: a car parking space, a seat on a crowded train, a delicious cup of tea, sitting next to your favourite colleague in the office.

    Think of the experiences that brighten your day, because there is an abundance of them. List them all and say thank you for each one. Be really detailed about what you write, and every day, keep adding to the list as you remember more and more things you recognise are blessings. You'll see that the more things you think of, the more your focus shifts from your challenges to your blessings.

2. The extraordinary things. These are the obstacles and challenges that appeared huge until we overcame them. These are the experiences that have shaped us and are now reference points in our life. They become an anchor, a testimony, a defining moment. When we reflect on our perseverance, we know that we are blessed and able to confront our next challenge. Say thank you for each one.

3. The opportunities. This may surprise you. Here, list your current challenges. We are thankful for these because, although they appear huge, we know from the things in the 'extraordinary' list above that these too, shall pass. We have utmost faith that from these tests will come testimonies from which we will learn and discover things we may not otherwise have.

"In all things and for all things, give thanks."

These experiences equip us with the tools to help others, which is the ultimate service. In life we are presented with God-ordained opportunities, ingeniously disguised as challenges or problems.

Be grateful for these experiences, because without them we would not have the experience of dealing with situations of this magnitude; we wouldn't have anything on which to hang our faith. It is from these situations that we learn and grow the most. Once we overcome them, the things on this list will become our reference point, our blueprint or survival guide to help not just ourselves in the future, but other people as well. Say thank you for them, recognising that things don't happen to you, they happen for you.

4. Create a daily practice of gratitude. After you've written down the list of everything you're grateful for, read this list every morning and evening, adding any more things you think of. Thank God for everything on the list. Express gratitude when you wake up in the morning and notice things to be grateful for throughout your day. What you feed your focus expands, so the more things you are grateful for, the more things you'll see to be grateful for.

5. Then take another piece of paper and on this sheet, write everything that's keeping you stuck, fearful, frustrated, lost, or trapped. Don't worry about how you'll overcome these, just list them out, writing what they are and how you feel about them.

"Begin each day with a grateful heart."

This is where the magic happens; the more you see things to be grateful for, you'll begin to see solutions to the challenges you are facing.

Whatever you feed your focus expands, so as long as you're focused on your challenges, you will see more challenges and this will make you feel even more stuck. The challenges will seem bigger; even small things seem bigger than they are because as you focus on them, they expand in your mind. When we focus on our blessings we see more blessings. In the words of Wayne Dyer, 'when we change the way we look at things, the things we look at change.' You cannot read the label when you're locked inside the box.

If you do these things, you'll change your whole life. You'll see that things will start to move from the challenges to the gratitude list. If you start this exercise at the beginning of the year, review your list at the end of the year and see how far you've come. You will be amazed by how much your life has changed, progressed, and improved, even though you may not necessarily have noticed the needle point moves on a day-to-day basis.

Say thank you for your goals and dreams, for the things you want in the next chapter of your life, as though you have already received them. Believe that they are making their way to you, and feel joy and gratitude for them.

What are you grateful for today? Gratitude leads to a happier, more content life. Say thank you hundreds of times each day.

"Thank You"

Goals

It's time to think about what you want in this next chapter of your life. Sit quietly, shut out all distractions, and listen to your heart. What arouses great desire in you? Wait until you hear from your heart. When your heart speaks, write your thoughts and desires. After this, take action towards creating your next chapter.

Start with the outcome in mind. Dream big, impossible dreams and break them down into realistic, attainable goals for each area of your life. These will serve as milestones towards the big goals. Write your goals in as much detail and clarity as possible. Be in a calm, peaceful, and serene state and develop a positive attitude about the accomplishment of your goals. Get excited about them and consider the following areas of your life: community, health and lifestyle, home, relationship, career, financial, and spiritual.

Write down everything you want in all of these areas, being as detailed as possible. Read your list every morning and night with expectation, with utmost faith and belief, and work toward your goals every day. Create an environment that empowers you through the things you love, including music, affirmations, and motivational messages.

"Do one thing every day that moves you closer to your dreams."

Exude positivity and gratitude for the assets you have which could bring you closer to your goals. Your current situation will open up to present great opportunities. Gratitude is the hook that keeps the door open for hope. Get a hook.

Have an attitude of gratitude and feel an abundance of fulfillment.

Goal-Setting Exercise

1. Write ten goals you want to achieve in the next twelve months from any of the different areas of your life.

2. Review the list and pick one goal which would make the biggest difference to your life. This is the goal you want to see in the next chapter of your life. It could be about your work, home, personal relationships, or family. This goal is the most significant and would have the greatest impact on your life. This is a major goal. Make it a big dream. It doesn't take any more effort to dream a big dream. Allow yourself to dream big. We'll call this your breakthrough goal. This is a goal which is a quantum leap. Write it in detail, clarify it, and believe it is possible. Don't let the evidence of your past control your future.

3. Set a deadline for accomplishing this goal. Don't worry about how or when you will achieve the goal. You have within you an inner GPS which will come up with the solutions you need and it will attract people, resources, and circumstances to help you.

"Setting goals before you know your purpose is like getting to the top of a ladder then realising that it is against the wrong wall."

- Jack Canfield

4. Make a list of everything you can think of that will propel you to achieve this goal.

5. Organise the list you created in order of sequence and priority.

6. Take action on your plan.

7. Do something every day that moves you towards accomplishing your goal.

8. Use the power of affirmations and visualisation to activate the subconscious mind and to strengthen your belief. Write an affirmation for your breakthrough goal as if you have already achieved it. The affirmation should be written in:

    a. The first person, so, 'I'

    b. The present tense, so, 'I am' instead of 'I will'

    c. In a positive or affirmative way, so 'I am at my ideal weight of...' instead of 'I am not overweight.'

9. Feel the excitement from the affirmation when you say it, as though it has already happened. For example:

    'I am so happy and grateful that I am at my ideal weight of [ideal weight] by [date] or sooner', instead of 'I am not overweight' or 'I have lost weight'.

Every morning and evening, visualise the goal as already complete. Feel the happiness, joy, relief, enthusiasm, etc. Your brain will try to release the thoughts because they are different from the beliefs you currently have. This is why you purposely intensify the process with affirmations to replace your current belief system so the brain complies once it knows you are committed to making a change.

"Goals without a plan are just dreams."

157

When you focus your vision consistently, you'll start seeing opportunities, ideas, people, resources, and circumstances to assist you. Things you've never seen before will start being presented to you. You will have creative ideas, increased motivation, and suggestions to act on. You should start and maintain action towards achieving your breakthrough goal. Say your affirmations in your hour of power every morning and again in the evening.

Take action! The inner work is critical but it needs to be backed up with taking action towards your goal. This is the outer work.

It must be borne in mind that the tragedy of life
doesn't lie in not reaching your goal.
The tragedy lies in having no goal to reach.
It isn't a calamity to die with dreams unfulfilled,
but it is a calamity not to dream.
It is not a disaster to be unable to capture your ideal
but it is a disaster to have no ideal to capture.
It is not a disgrace not to reach the stars,
but it is a disgrace to have no stars to reach for.
Not failure, but low aim, is sin.

- Dr. Benjamin Mays, 1894 - 1984

Service

Acts of service to humanity give us meaning, happiness, and contentment. They remind us that we are a part of something bigger than ourselves and bring us a genuine sense of purpose and fulfillment.

When you give, you become a channel for love and light to the world, which helps you create more love in your life. You feel more alive and able to sustain life. It is a cycle; the more you give, the more you'll get.

To be fulfilled, find a cause you identify with and give your time to develop or mentor others and share your gifts with the world. You were given a gift, and now it's time to pass that gift along to someone else. Share your gift by serving it to the world, one person at a time. Give your time, give your money, and give your knowledge. Whatever you give, give it freely. You'll get more in return.

Inspire others because when you do, you inspire yourself. Love, hope, happiness, inspiration, and motivation are perfumes you sprinkle on others and can't help getting some on yourself.

"A candle loses nothing by lighting another candle."
- James Keller, 1900 - 1977

Silence

With the noise and distractions in the world, it is necessary to be still and silent so that we can communicate with our hearts. Our hearts speak to us in whispers and we often do not hear unless we are silent. Then, when we are spiritually awake to receive instructions from within, with amazing clarity and precision, we are guided to people, places and resources who need our help or who can help us. Such is the power we have within us, but often it is left untapped because we do not recognise what we possess. The answers lie inside you. All you need to do is look, listen, and trust.

Take time out to reflect and consider your goals. In what areas is further development required and where have you honed your skills?

Ensure you are taking care of your physical and mental wellbeing so you are able to work towards your goals and be at your best.

Develop habits which fulfill you and support the achievement of your goals.

"Silence is golden."

Meditation

Meditation has been described as the master key to our mind, our heart, and our spirit because it can open doors. It is a highly effective practice for connecting with our higher power. It helps to clear the mind of all the noise and allows us to just be. Afterwards, you will find that you have a new level of clarity.

Meditation is not a state where we work on dreams, but as we open ourselves up to our hearts, we are able to get clarity and responses which manifest our desires. As we quiet the mind, we connect with our inner power to manifest our already-stated desires.

Exercise
1. Every day, for 10 to 15 minutes, wear comfortable clothes and sit somewhere quiet where you will not be interrupted or distracted. Close your eyes and take deep breaths in for 10 seconds and deep breaths out for 10 seconds. Let go of all thoughts and focus on nothing else except your breathing.
2. At first your brain will try to distract you with thoughts. That's normal, it's not used to letting go. Don't fight it or you'll come out of your meditative state. Acknowledge the thoughts, then gently release them, letting them go. They will stop after a while and you'll start to slip away, entering a state where the world slips away. That's where you'll find true quiet.

"The quieter you get, the more you hear."

3. When you come out of the meditative state, allow yourself time to get back in sync with the world and space around you. In your journal, write whatever thoughts, instructions, or messages that come to you.

Do not be discouraged if you struggle to clear your mind when you first start to meditate. It gets easier with practice and you'll get some benefit even with small steps.

"The answers you seek don't come when the mind is busy.
They come when the mind is still."
- Unknown

Mindfulness

Mindfulness means deliberately focusing attention on the present, or 'being in the moment'. We can get so caught up with the preoccupations of life: fixating on our to-do lists, worrying about the future, or regretting the past, that we lose connection with the present. The result is a feeling of unease, overwhelming stress, and depression. These feelings can impact our physical and mental health and our overall wellbeing.

In order to experience the blessings and joys of your life, you need to allow yourself to be present. This way you will move from struggling to thriving, and from being overwhelmed and stressed to being happy, empowered, present, and bursting with unfolding potential.

Exercise

1. Sit quietly and focus on your natural breathing. Feel yourself breathe, hold it for a moment, and then breathe out. Allow thoughts to come and go from your mind without judgment and return your focus to your breath.
2. Notice sensations in and around you. Look at them and let them pass. It is important to listen without judgment. Simply be aware of your surroundings, and process sensations as they happen. This will help to clear your mind and listen to your intuition instead of thinking about daily tasks, your past, or your future.

"It all starts with a dream."

Mindfulness is about accepting whatever arises in your consciousness at each moment. It involves being kind and forgiving toward yourself. Try to practice mindfulness daily, for 10 to 20 minutes.

"As you start to walk on the way, the way appears."
- Rumi, 1207 - 1273

Scripting

Scripting or journaling is a powerful way of ensuring you become the hero of your story for the rest of your life. It allows you to write all your emotions and thoughts, reflect on your feelings, and store your memories.

Scripting allows us to quiet the world around us and tune in to our hearts. When you put a pen in your hand and you start writing without any real agenda, you'll find that your inner self emerges. You'll write thoughts that you didn't even know you had and you'll learn about yourself in the process. With your attention turned inward, your true self will be revealed in every word you put on paper.

You do not need to think about what to write or how to start. Allow your mind to wander and let your heart take the wheel and take you on a journey. Don't force it. Don't think about how it sounds or looks. Don't worry if you're not a great writer. Your heart will do the talking. Just listen and write what you hear.

If you're more comfortable typing, then do so. When you spend time in quiet contemplation and mindfulness, handwriting is a powerful way of connecting with and distilling your inner self.

"The best way to predict your future is to create it."
- Abraham Lincoln, 1809 - 1865

After a few weeks, review what you've written and take note of the emerging patterns and recurring thoughts. Identify your desires and any limiting mindset beliefs that arise.

Scripting is also a great way to discover your utmost desires and limitations. You will recognise when you are not thinking positively and will begin the habit of talking about things the way you would like them to be.

Exercise

1. Find the most beautiful pen.
2. Get a beautiful, unused journal. There is a journal available as part of a bundle with this book.
3. Start writing. What do you write? Anything that comes to your mind: your thoughts about your day, the day ahead, your future, your desires, your feelings.

If you're still unsure, here are some prompts to get you started:

- What does living a fulfilled life mean to me?
- What does my ideal day look like?
- What are my values and what is important to me?
- How can I nurture my soul?
- What advice would I give myself?
- When do I feel happiest and most in tune with myself?
- How can I serve others and contribute to the world?

"What do you dream about doing, being, or having?"

Asking For Help

We all need help sometimes. Asking for help is not a sign of weakness, and it can sometimes be the difference between success and failure. It shows that you are self-aware, confident in your skills and abilities, and willing to learn something new. It builds resilience and mental resolve. Asking for help is rewarding for the helper because they get to share their knowledge and skills, and it boosts their self-esteem.

When you ask for help, you inspire others to do the same. Look for opportunities to help others and add value to their lives, while you seek help from others. Helping others opens up possibilities for you because you get back what you put out. Asking for help is not giving up, it is a sign that you don't want to give up.

Some people won't ask for help because of pride or ego. Don't allow ego to stop you from reaching your destiny. Remember that no man is an island; we all need help sometimes.

Forgiveness

When you forgive, your forgiveness is not just about others, it is also about you. By forgiving, you release yourself from the mental bondage of holding on to the negative feelings associated with the circumstances. Develop the self-compassion and self-empathy to navigate out of it. When you do, you regain power over the situation because you are no longer emotionally attached to it. Whatever has happened in the past should remain there. Focus on the now, the present. Let it go!

Often, when we think about our experiences, we are overly critical, judgmental, and lacking in compassion or empathy. Give yourself permission to make mistakes and allow yourself to rebound so you can soar again. Let it go!

Learn the lesson from the mistake and move on. Forgive everyone, including yourself. Let it go!

"Don't cling onto a mistake because you spent a lot of time making it."

Lord grant me the serenity
to accept the things I cannot change,
the courage to change the things that I can,
and the wisdom to know the difference.
- Reinhold Niebuhr, 1892 – 1971

Accept Responsibility

Accepting responsibility for your life is about control and not about blame. When you take control, you regain power over your life. Do not blame others or circumstances for your life, or you will hand over control of your happiness. The only person responsible for your happiness is you. Handing it over to anyone else is mental bondage. Determine to be the master of your fate and not the victim of your circumstances. If you don't take control of your life, someone else will.

While you might not be responsible for your circumstances, you should choose your response to them. This is how you accept responsibility. Take charge of where you are and where you want to go in life. It requires courage, but it also builds confidence, puts you firmly in control to regain power, and shapes the outcome of your life.

Responsibility frees you from mental burden, allowing you to focus on your happiness, health, wealth, and emotional wellbeing. Regardless of the past, the future lies ahead with an open slate, waiting for you to take control and create a wonderful life. Accept responsibility for your life, embrace your uniqueness, and regain your power, self-reliance, and self-respect. Blame no one and forgive everyone, including yourself.

"He who blames others has a long way to go on his journey.
He who blames himself is halfway there.
He who blames no one has arrived."
- Unknown

Vision Boards

A vision board is a powerful visualisation tool to tell your mind what you desire. It is an inspirational collage that represents your vision of your goals, your dreams, your future. Whatever you focus on, you attract. So, if you put your goals on a vision board and look at it regularly, the constant observance of the images sends messages of your dreams and desires to your mind, which sets about arranging people and resources to recreate the images in reality.

You can also create an actual or digital vision book. A book has the advantage of being more private and easier to carry, such as when travelling.

Whether you're creating a vision board or a vision book, the process is the same.

1. Create your beliefs—your dreams and goals of your ideal life. Have a mental picture of what you want to experience in life and write it down. Be so detailed and descriptive that if someone were to read your list, they would have a similar mental picture of your desires. Open your imagination; write anything you want in every area of your life. Don't hold back; this is your life.

"The best dreams happen when we're awake."

2. Get a vision board (with supplies for sticking pictures to it), a vision book, or create your vision board digitally (Canva is great for this). Gather magazines and go through them, cutting out pictures that represent the life and dreams you want. Once cut out, stick the pictures on your board or into your book.

3. Every morning and every night, read your list and look at your vision board. Allow yourself to feel as though you are already living your dream. Feel the happiness, feel the love, feel the joy.

4. Get working towards your dreams, no matter how small the steps. Don't worry about how you're going to get what you want, just start working towards it. People and resources behind the scenes will make your dreams happen. You just need to do your part. Get to work.

5. Watch it happen.

Review your list regularly and cross things off as you achieve them. Oh, don't forget to say thank you for your accomplishments. Update your list as you grow and receive blessings.

> *"Write the vision and make it plain on tables,*
> *that he may run that readeth it."*
> - Holy Bible, KJV, Habakkuk 2:2

"Focus on the rainbow,
don't think about the pot of gold
at the end of your journey.
The rainbow is made of diamonds."
- Unknown

You have reached the end of the book but not the end of the journey. This is the beginning of the next part of the journey. Don't focus on the destination; the beauty is not in the destination but in the journey.

I would like to invite you to continue the journey with me by joining my online community at:

- Website: https://www.ziano.co.uk
- Instagram: https://www.instagram.com/ziano_mindspa
- Facebook: https://www.facebook.com/ene.obi.7
- LinkedIn: https://www.linkedin.com/in/eneobi/

Printed in Great Britain
by Amazon